Foundation For Faith

by Derek Prince

"For other foundation can no man lay than that is laid, which is Jesus Christ."

I Corinthians 3:11

"Whosoever cometh to me, and heareth my sayings, and doeth them, I will shew you to whom he is like: he is like a man which built an house, and digged deep, and laid the foundation on a rock."

Luke 6:47,48

ISBN 0-934920-00-1

TABLE OF CONTENTS

DEREK PRINCE

King's Scholar, Eton College
B.A., M.A. Cambridge
Formerly
Fellow of King's College,
Cambridge

ABOUT THE AUTHOR

Derek Prince was born in India, of British parents. He was educated as a scholar of Greek and Latin at two of Britain's most famous educational institutions - Eton College and Cambridge University. From 1940 to 1949, he held a Fellowship (equivalent to a resident professorship) in Ancient and Modern Philosophy at King's College, Cambridge. He also studied Hebrew and Aramaic, both at Cambridge University and at the Hebrew University in Jerusalem. In addition, he speaks a number of other modern languages.

In the early years of World War II, while serving as a hospital attendant with the British Army, Derek Prince experienced a life-changing encounter with Jesus Christ, concerning which, he writes:

> Out of this encounter, I formed two conclusions which I have never since had reason to change: first, that Jesus Christ is alive; second, that the Bible is a true, relevant, up-to-date book. These two conclusions radically and permanently altered the whole course of my life.

At the end of World War II, he remained where the British Army had placed him - in Jerusalem. Through his marriage to his first wife, Lydia, he became father to the eight adopted girls in Lydia's children's home there. Together, the family saw the rebirth of the State of Israel in 1948. While serving as educator in Kenya, Derek and Lydia adopted their ninth child, an African baby girl. Lydia died in 1975, and Derek Prince married his present wife, Ruth, in 1978.

In the intervening years, Derek Prince has served as pastor, educator, lecturer, and counselor on several continents, and is internationally recognized as one of the leading Bible expositors of our time. He has authored over 20 books, many of which have been translated into other languages. In great demand as a conference speaker, Derek Prince travels frequently to many other parts of the world, and also maintains a base in Israel.

Non-denominational and non-sectarian in his approach, Derek Prince has prophetic insight into the significance of current events in the light of Bible prophecy.

* * * * *

With a few changes, these messages are printed here exactly as they were delivered over the air on the Study Hour radio program.

I
What is the Foundation of the Christian Faith?

Christ The Rock - Confrontation - Revelation -
Acknowledgment - Confession

Welcome to the Study Hour.

Our textbook - the Bible.

Our subject today - "Foundations."

Our aim - today and every day - **not** to tell you what to believe - but so to direct you in your own study of the Bible that you may be able to form your own conclusions as to what it really teaches.

Without question, the Bible is by far the most widely read and the most influential book in the entire history of the human race. We believe, therefore, that every educated, intelligent person today has an obligation to study the Bible for himself, to find out what it really teaches and wherein lies the reason for its immense and abiding impact upon the human race. This applies both to those who profess Christianity and to those who do not. Far too many people today tend to dismiss the Bible without ever having given it any serious study. On the other hand, far too many professing Christians accept without proper examination the views or the doctrines of some particular church or group with which they happen to be associated. As a result, their religious life lacks any real depth or purpose, and they are never in a position to give to others a clear or convincing account of what they believe or why they believe it.

We urge you therefore, and we challenge you, to accept the Bible's own challenge - to study for yourself.

Stay with us now as we study this most important subject - "Foundations."

* * *

In various places the Bible compares the life of a believer to the construction of a building, or an edifice. For instance, in the Epistle of Jude, verse 20, we read: "Building up yourselves on your most holy faith." The apostle Paul also uses the same picture in various places. In First Corinthians, chapter 3, verses 9 and 10, he says: "Ye are God's building.

As a wise master builder, I have laid the foundation." In Ephesians chapter 2, verse 22, he says: "Ye also are builded together for an habitation of God through the Spirit." In Colossians, chapter 2, verse 7, he says: "Rooted and built up in Christ, and stablished in the faith." In Acts, chapter 20, verse 32, speaking to the elders of the church at Ephesus, he says: "The word of God's grace is able to build you up." In all these passages, the believer's life is compared to the construction of a building.

Now, in the natural order, the first and most important feature of any solid and permanent building is the foundation. The foundation necessarily sets a limit to the weight and height of the building which is to be erected upon it. A weak foundation can only support a small building. A strong foundation can support a large building. There is a fixed relationship between the foundation and the building.

In the city of Jerusalem I once lived in a house that had been built by an Assyrian. This man had obtained from the municipality a license to build a house of two stories, and the foundation was laid accordingly. However, in order to increase his income from renting the building, this Assyrian had built on a third story, without obtaining permission to do so. The result was that, while we were actually living in the house, the whole building began to settle down on one corner, and eventually went right out of perpendicular. What was the reason for this? Just this - the foundation was not strong enough to support the house which that man tried to erect upon it.

Even so in the spiritual order, the same thing happens in the lives of many professing Christians. They set out with every intention of raising a fine, imposing edifice of Christianity in their lives. But alas, before long their fine edifice begins to sink, to sag, to get out of true. It leans grotesquely. Sometimes it even collapses completely, and leaves nothing but a ruined heap of vows and prayers and good intentions which have gone unfulfilled.

Beneath this mass of ruins the reason for the failure lies buried. It was the foundation, which was never properly laid, and which was unable to support the fine edifice which it was proposed to erect.

* * *

What, then, is God's appointed foundation for the Christian life?

The answer is clearly given by the apostle Paul in First Corinthians, chapter 3, verse 11: "Other foundation can no man lay than that is laid, which is Jesus Christ."

This is confirmed also by the apostle Peter in his First Epistle, chapter 2, verse 6, where Peter speaks of Jesus Christ, and says: "Wherefore also it is contained in the scripture, Behold, I lay in Zion a chief corner stone, elect, precious." The scripture to which Peter here refers is found in the prophet Isaiah chapter 28, verse 16, where it says: "Therefore, thus saith the Lord God, Behold, I lay in Zion for a foundation, a stone, a tried stone, a precious corner stone, a sure foundation."

Thus Old Testament and New Testament alike agree in this vital fact: The true foundation of the Christian life is Jesus Christ Himself - nothing else, and no one else. It is not a creed, not a church, not a denomination, not an ordinance or a ceremony. It is Jesus Christ Himself - and "other foundation can no man lay."

In this connection it is helpful also to consider the words of Jesus Himself. In Matthew's Gospel, chapter 16, verses 13 to 18, we read the following conversation between Jesus and His disciples: "When Jesus came into the coasts of Caesarea Philippi, he asked his disciples, saying, Whom do men say that I the Son of man am? And they said, Some say that thou art John the Baptist: some, Elias; and others, Jeremias, or one of the prophets. He saith unto them, But whom say ye that I am? And Simon Peter answered and said, Thou art the Christ, the Son of the living God. And Jesus answered and said unto him, Blessed art thou, Simon Bar-jona: for flesh and blood hath not revealed it unto thee, but my Father which is in heaven. And I say also unto thee, that thou art Peter, and upon this rock I will build my church; and the gates of hell shall not prevail against it."

Now it has sometimes been suggested that these words of Jesus mean that the apostle Peter is the rock upon which the Christian church is to be built, and thus that Peter is in some sense the foundation of Christianity rather than Christ Himself. This question of the true foundation is of such vital and far reaching importance that it is desirable to examine the words of Jesus very carefully, in order to make sure of their proper meaning.

In the original Greek of the New Testament there is, in the answer of Christ to Peter, a deliberate play upon words. In Greek, the name "Peter" is **Petros**, the word for "rock" is **petra**. Playing upon this similarity in sound, Jesus says: "Thou art Peter (**Petros**), and upon this rock (**petra**), I will build my church."

Though there is a similarity in sound between these two words, their meaning is quite different. **Petros** means a small stone, or a pebble. **Petra** means a large rock. The idea of building a church upon a pebble would obviously be ridiculous, and therefore could not be Christ's real meaning.

There is one modern language in which it is possible, even in translation, to retain something of this play upon words. That language is French. The French form of the name "Peter" is **Pierre**. In French, **pierre** also means a stone. On the other hand, the French word for rock is **rocher**. Thus, in the French version of the New Testament, Jesus says to Peter: "Thou art Peter--**Pierre**--a stone, and upon this rock--**rocher**--I will build my church."

In this way, the French version brings out the same point as the original Greek: Jesus is not **identifying** Peter with the rock; on the contrary, He is **contrasting** Peter with the rock. He is pointing out how small and insignificant the little stone, Peter, is in comparison to the great rock upon which the church is to be built.

Common sense and scripture alike confirm this fact. If the church of Christ were really founded upon the apostle Peter, it would surely be the most insecure and unstable edifice in the world. Just a little further on in the same chapter of Matthew's Gospel, we read that Jesus began to forewarn His disciples of His impending rejection and crucifixion. The account then continues:

"Then Peter took him, and began to rebuke him, saying, Be it far from thee, Lord: this shall not be unto thee. But he (Christ) turned, and said unto Peter, Get thee behind me, Satan: thou art in an offence unto me; for thou savourest not the things that be of God, but those that be of men."

Here, Christ directly charges Peter with being influenced in his thinking by the opinions of men, and even by the promptings of Satan himself. How could such a man be the foundation of the entire Christian church?

Later on in the gospels we read that, rather than confess Christ before a serving maid, Peter publicly denied his Lord three times.

Even after the resurrection and the day of Pentecost, Paul tells us, in Galatians, chapter 2, verses 11 to 14, that Peter was influenced by fear of his countrymen to compromise at one point concerning the truth of the gospel.

Surely then, Peter was no rock. He was lovable, impetuous but a man just like the rest, with all the inherent weaknesses and failings of humanity. The only rock upon which true and stable Christian faith can be based is Christ Himself.

Plain confirmation of this vital fact concerning the foundation of all true, scriptural faith is found also in the Old Testament.

In Psalm 18, verse 2, the psalmist David, prophetically inspired by the Holy Spirit, says this: "The Lord is my rock...in whom I will trust; my buckler, and the horn of my salvation, and my high tower."

In Psalm 62 David again makes a similar confession of faith. In verses 1 and 2 he says: "Truly my soul waiteth upon God: from him cometh my salvation. He only is my rock and my salvation; he is my defence; I shall not be greatly moved." Again in verses 5, 6 and 7 of the same Psalm, David says: "My soul, wait thou only upon God... He only is my rock and my salvation; he is my defence; I shall not be moved. In God is my salvation and my glory: the rock of my strength, and my refuge, is in God."

Nothing could be plainer than that. Notice the emphatic repetition of the word "only," which occurs three times in six verses. In the same six verses, the word "rock" occurs four times, and the word "salvation" occurs five times. That is to say, the word "rock" and the word "salvation" are by the scripture intimately and inseparably joined. Each is found only in one person, and that person is the Lord Himself.

If anyone should require yet further confirmation of this, we may turn to the words of Peter himself. In Acts, chapter 4, verse 12, speaking to the people of Israel concerning Jesus Christ of Nazareth, Peter says: "Neither is there salvation in any other: for there is none other name under heaven given among men, whereby we must be saved."

The Lord Jesus Christ, therefore, Himself alone, is the true rock, the rock of ages, in whom there is salvation. The person who builds upon this foundation can say, like David:

"He only is my rock and my salvation: he is my defence;
I shall not be moved."

*   *   *

How then does a person begin to build upon this rock,
which is Christ?

Let us turn back again to that dramatic moment when
Christ and Peter stood face to face, and Peter said: "Thou
art the Christ, the Son of the living God." Let us see for
ourselves exactly what transpired between them.

We have seen that the rock is Christ Himself. But it is
not Christ in isolation or in abstraction. There was a definite
personal experience on the part of Peter. We may analyse
four successive stages in this experience of Peter:

First, there was a direct, personal confrontation of
Peter by Christ. Christ and Peter stood face to face. There
was no mediator between them. No other human being played
any part at all in the experience.

Second, there was a direct, personal revelation granted
to Peter. Jesus said to Peter: "Flesh and blood hath not revealed it unto thee, but my Father which is in heaven."
This was not the outcome of natural reasoning or of intellectual understanding. It was the outcome of a direct spiritual
revelation to Peter by God the Father Himself.

Third, there was a personal acknowledgment by Peter
of the truth which had thus been revealed to him.

Fourth, there was an open and public confession by
Peter of the truth which he acknowledged.

In these four successive stages we see what it means to
build upon the rock. There is nothing purely abstract, or
intellectual, or theoretical, about the whole thing. In each
stage, there is a definite, individual experience.

The first stage is a direct, personal confrontation of
Christ. The second stage is a direct, spiritual revelation of
Christ. The third stage is a personal acknowledgment of
Christ. The fourth stage is an open and personal confession
of Christ.

It is Christ thus experienced, Christ thus revealed, Christ
thus acknowledged and confessed--it is Christ who in this
way becomes for each individual believer the rock upon
which his faith is built.

The question arises: Is such an experience possible today?
Can a person today come to know Christ in the same direct
and personal way that Peter came to know Him then?

To this important question we must answer "Yes," for the following two reasons:

First, it was not Christ in His purely human nature who was revealed to Peter: Peter already knew Jesus of Nazareth, the carpenter's son. The one who was now revealed to Peter was the divine, eternal, unchanging Son of God. This is the same Christ who now lives exalted in heaven at the Father's right hand. In the passage of nearly two thousand years, there has been no change in Him at all. It is still "Jesus Christ, the same yesterday, and today, and forever." As He was revealed then to Peter, He can still be revealed today to those who sincerely seek Him.

Second, the revelation did not come by "flesh and blood"-- it did not come by any physical or sensory means. It was a spiritual revelation, the work of God's own Holy Spirit. The same Spirit who gave this revelation to Peter is now at work in all the world, revealing the same Christ. Jesus Himself promised His disciples, in John's Gospel, chapter 16, verses 13 and 14: "When he, the Spirit of truth, is come, he will guide you into all truth...He shall glorify me: for he shall receive of mine and shall show it unto you."

Since the entire revelation is in the eternal, spiritual realm, it is not limited in any way by material or physical factors, such as the passage of time, or the change of language, or customs, or clothing, or circumstances.

This individual and personal experience of Jesus Christ the Son of God, by the Holy Spirit revealed, acknowledged, and confessed, remains the one true unchanging rock, the one unmovable foundation, upon which all true Christian faith must be based. Creeds and opinions, churches and denominations--all these may change, but this one true rock of God's salvation by personal faith in Christ remains eternal and unchanging. Upon it a person may build his faith for time and for eternity with a security and confidence which nothing can ever overthrow.

* * *

Nothing is more striking, in the writings and testimony of the early Christians, than their serenity and confidence concerning their faith in Christ.

In John's Gospel, chapter 17, verse 3, we read: "This is life eternal, that they might know thee the only true God, and Jesus Christ, whom thou hast sent." This is not merely to know God in a general way through nature or conscience, as Creator or Judge. This is to know God revealed personally in Jesus Christ. Neither is it to know about Jesus Christ, as merely a historical character or a great teacher. It is to know Christ Himself, directly and personally, and God in Him.

Again, in the First Epistle of John chapter 5, verse 13, the apostle writes: "These things have I written unto you that believe on the name of the Son of God; that ye may know that ye have eternal life." The early Christians not merely believed, they also knew. They had a kind of experiential faith which produced a definite knowledge of that which they believed.

A little further on, in verse 20 of the same chapter, the apostle John writes again: "We know that the Son of God is come, and hath given us an understanding, that we may know him that is true, and we are in him that is true, even in his Son Jesus Christ."

Note the humble, yet serene confidence of these words. Their basis is knowledge of a person, and that person in Jesus Christ Himself.

The apostle Paul gave the same kind of personal testimony, in Second Timothy, chapter 1, verse 12, when he said: "I know whom I have believed, and am persuaded that he is able to keep that which I have committed unto him against that day." Notice that Paul did not say, "I know what I have believed." He said, "I know whom I have believed." His faith was not founded upon a creed or a church, but upon a person, whom he knew by direct acquaintance, and that person was Jesus Christ. As a result of this personal acquaintance with Christ, he had a serene confidence concerning the well-being of his soul, which nothing in time or eternity could overthrow.

For a number of years I used to conduct regular street meetings in the great city of London, England. At the close of such meetings I would sometimes approach people who had stood listening to the message, and ask them this simple question: "Are you a Christian?" Many times I would receive answers such as these: "I think so" or "I hope so" or "I try to be" or "I don't know." All those who give answers like these betray plainly one fact: their faith is not build upon the one sure foundation of a direct personal knowledge of Jesus Christ.

Suppose I were to put that same question to you, my friend: "Are you a Christian?" What kind of answer would you be able to give?

May I close our study by a word of advice which is found in the book of Job, chapter 22, verse 21: "Acquaint now thyself with him, and be at peace: thereby good shall come unto thee."

* * *

In our next study we shall continue to examine in a very practical way this vital question: How you can build upon the foundation of Jesus Christ in your life.

II
How to Build on the Foundation

The Bible - Foundation Of Faith - Proof Of Discipleship - Test Of Love - Means Of Revelation

Welcome to the Study Hour.

Our textbook--the Bible.

Our subject today--"Foundations"--the second study in this most important series.

Once again, we urge you and we challenge you: accept the Bible's own challenge--study for yourself.

In the first study in the series, "Foundations," we asked the question: What is the basic foundation of all Christian faith and experience? Our answer was that the foundation is none other than Jesus Christ Himself, made real to the believer in a direct, personal encounter. In this basic experience, we analyzed the following four successive stages: first, a direct personal confrontation of Christ; second, a direct spiritual revelation of Christ in His divine, eternal nature as the Son of God; third, a personal acknowledgment of the truth thus revealed; and fourth, an open and public confession of this truth.

The question which we shall now examine in our second study is this: Once we have laid in our own lives the foundation of this personal encounter with Christ, in what way can we continue thereafter to build upon this foundation? Or, more briefly, our question is: How to build upon the foundation, once laid?

* * *

The answer to this question is found in the well-known parable about the wise man and the foolish man, each of whom built a house, related for us by Christ in Matthew's Gospel, chapter 7, verses 24-27:

"Therefore, whosoever heareth these sayings of mine, and doeth them, I will liken him unto a wise man, which built his house upon a rock: And the rain descended, and the floods came, and the winds blew, and beat upon that house; and it fell not: for it was founded upon a rock. And every one that heareth these sayings of mine, and doeth them not, shall be likened unto a foolish man, which built his house upon the sand: And the rain descended, and the floods came, and the winds blew, and beat upon that house; and it fell: and great was the fall of it."

Notice carefully that the difference between these men did not lie in the tests to which their houses were subjected. Each man's house alike had to endure the storm--the wind, the rain, the floods. Christianity has never offered anyone a storm-free passage to heaven. On the contrary, in Acts chapter 14, verse 22, we are warned that"we must through much tribulation enter into the kingdom of God." Any road signposted to "Heaven," which by-passes tribulation, is a deception. It will not lead to the promised destination.

What, then, was the real difference between the two men and their houses? The answer is that the wise man built upon a foundation of rock, the foolish man upon a foundation of sand. The wise man built in such a way that his house came through the storm unmoved and secure; the foolish man built in such a way that his house could not weather the storm.

Just what are we to understand by this picture of building upon a rock? Just what does it mean for each of us as Christians, in plain, simple language? Christ Himself makes this very plain, for He says: "Whosoever **heareth these sayings of mine, and doeth them,** I will liken him unto a wise man, which built his house upon a rock." Thus, building upon the rock consists precisely in this: hearing and doing the words of Christ.

Once the foundation of Christ Himself, the Rock, has been laid in our lives, thereafter we build upon that foundation by hearing and doing the Word of God--that is, by diligently studying and applying in our lives the teaching of God's Word. It was for this reason that the apostle Paul said, in Acts chapter 20, verse 32, to the elders of the church at Ephesus: "And now, brethren, I commend you to God, and to the **word of his grace,** which is able to **build you up...**" It is God's Word, and God's Word alone--as we hear it and do it, as we study it and apply it--which is able to build up within us as believers, a strong, secure edifice of faith, laid upon the foundation of Christ Himself.

This brings us to a subject of supreme importance in the Christian faith: that is, the relationship between Christ and the Bible; and, arising out of this, the relationship of each Christian to the Bible.

Continually throughout its pages the Bible declares itself to be the "Word of God." On the other hand, there are a number of passages in the scriptures where the same title-- the Word, or the Word of God-- is given to Jesus Christ Himself. For example, in John's Gospel, chapter 1, verse 1, "In the beginning was the Word, and the Word was with God, and the Word was God." In John chapter 1, verse 14, "And the Word was made flesh, and dwelt among us, (and we beheld his glory, the glory as of the only begotten of the Father)." Again, in Revelation chapter 19, verse 13, "He (Christ) was clothed with a vesture dipped in blood: and his name is called The Word of God."

This identity of name reveals an identity of nature. The Bible is the Word of God, and Christ is the Word of God. Each alike is a divine, authoritative, perfect revelation of God. Each agrees perfectly with the other. The Bible perfectly reveals Christ; Christ perfectly fulfils the Bible. The Bible is the written Word of God; Christ is the living Word of God. Before His incarnation, Christ was the eternal Word with the Father. In His incarnation, Christ is the Word made flesh. The same Holy Spirit that reveals God through His written Word, the Bible, reveals God in the Word made flesh, as Jesus of Nazareth.

If Christ is in this sense perfectly one with the Bible, then it follows that the relationship of the believer to the Bible must be the same as his relationship to Christ. To this fact the scriptures bear testimony in many places.

Let us turn first to the fourteenth chapter of John's Gospel. In this chapter Jesus is warning His disciples that He is about to be taken from them in bodily presence, and that thereafter there must be a new kind of relationship and fellowship between Him and them. The disciples are unable and unwilling to accept or to understand this impending change. In particular, they are unable to understand how, if Christ is about to go away from them, they will still be able to see Him or have communion with Him, after He has left them.

In verse 19, Christ says: "Yet a little while, and the world seeth me no more; but ye see me"--or we might render it--"but ye shall continue to see me."

Because of this statement by Jesus, Judas (not Iscariot, but the other Judas) asks, in verse 22: "Lord, how is it that thou wilt manifest thyself unto us, and not unto the world?" In other words: "Lord, if you are going away, and if the world will see you no more, by what means will you still be able to manifest yourself to us, your disciples, but not to the world--that is, to those who are not your disciples? What kind of communication will you be able to maintain with us, which will not be open to the world?"

In verse 23, Jesus answers this question and says: "If a man love me, he will keep my words: and my Father will love him, and we will come unto him, and make our abode with him."

The key to the proper understanding of this answer is found in the phrase "he will **keep my words.**" The main feature which distinguishes a true disciple from the people of the world is that a true disciple is one who **keeps Christ's words.**

If we now relate Christ's answer here given to the original question, "Lord, how wilt thou manifest thyself unto us, and not unto the world?", we find revealed in this answer four facts of absolutely vital importance for every person who sincerely desires to be a real Christian.

For the sake of absolute clarity, let me first repeat the answer of Jesus in verse 23: "If a man love me, he will keep my words: and my Father will love him; and we will come unto him, and make our abode with him."

Here, then, are the four vital facts concerning God's Word, which are revealed by Christ's answer: First, the keeping of God's Word is the supreme distinguishing feature which marks out the disciple of Christ from the rest of the world; second, the keeping of God's Word is the supreme test of the disciple's love for God, and the supreme cause of God's love for the disciple; third, it is through God's Word, as it is kept and obeyed, that Christ manifests Himself to the disciple; fourth, it is through God's Word that the Father and the Son together come into the life of the disciple and establish their enduring abode with him.

Side by side with this answer of Christ, let me set the words of the apostle John in the First Epistle of John, chapter 2, verses 4 and 5: "He that saith, I know him, and keepeth not his commandments, is a liar, and the truth is not in him. But whoso **keepeth his word,** in him verily is the love of God perfected: hereby know we that we are in him."

We see from these two passages that it is absolutely impossible to overestimate, or overemphasize, the importance of the place of God's Word in the life of the Christian believer.

Let me present these truths to you in a direct and personal way: The keeping of God's Word is the supreme distinguishing feature which should mark you out from the world as a disciple of Christ. It is the test of your love for God. It is the cause of God's love and favour toward you. It is the way that Christ will manifest Himself to you. It is the way that God the Father and God the Son will come into your life and make their abode with you.

Let me put it to you in this way:

Your attitude toward God's Word is your attitude toward God Himself. You do not love God more than you love His Word. You do not obey God more than you obey His Word. You do not honour God more than you honour His Word. You do not have more room in your heart and life for God than you have for His Word.

Do you want to know how much God means to you? You can easily find out. Just ask yourself, How much does God's Word mean to me? The answer to the second question is the answer also to the first. God means as much to you as His Word means to you--just that much, and no more.

* * *

There is today a general and ever increasing awareness among all sections of the Christian Church that we have entered into the period of time foretold in Acts chapter 2, verse 17: "And it shall come to pass in the last days, saith God, I will pour out of my Spirit upon all flesh: and your sons and your daughters shall prophesy, and your young men shall see visions, and your old men shall dream dreams." I am humbly grateful to God that in recent years I have been privileged to experience and to observe, at first hand, outpourings of the Spirit of God in four different continents--in Africa, in Asia, in Europe, and in America--in which every detail of this prophecy has been enacted and repeated many times over. As a consequence, I believe firmly in the scriptural manifestation in these days of all nine gifts of the Holy Spirit; I believe that God speaks to His believing people through prophecies, visions, dreams, and other forms of supernatural revelation.

Nevertheless, I hold most firmly that the scriptures are the supreme, authoritative means by which, above all others, God speaks to His people, reveals Himself to His people, guides and directs His people. I hold that all other forms of revelation must be carefully proved by reference to the scriptures, and accepted only insofar as they accord with the doctrines, precepts, practices and examples set forth in the scriptures.

In First Thessalonians chapter 5, verses 19, 20 and 21 we are told: "Quench not the Spirit. Despise not prophesyings. Prove all things; hold fast that which is good." It is wrong, therefore, to quench any genuine manifestation of the Holy Spirit. It is wrong to despise any prophesying given through the Holy Spirit. On the other hand, it is vitally necessary to prove--to test, to check--any manifestation of the Spirit, or any prophesying, by reference to the standard of the scriptures, and thereafter to hold fast--to accept, to retain--only those manifestations or prophesyings which are in full accord with this divine standard.

Again, in Isaiah chapter 8, verse 20, we are told: "To the law and to the testimony: if they speak not according to this word, it is because there is no light in them." (An alternative translation is: "If they speak not according to this word, they are not to be sought unto.") Thus the scripture--the Word of God--is the supreme standard by which all else must be judged and tested. No doctrine, no practice, no prophecy, no revelation is to be accepted if it is not in full accord with the Word of God. No person, no group, no organization, no church has authority to change, to override, or to depart from the Word of God. In whatever respect or whatever degree any person, any group, any organization or any church departs from the Word of God, in that respect and in that degree they are in darkness--there is no light in them-- they are not to be sought unto.

We are living in a time when it is urgently and increasingly necessary to emphasize the supremacy and the preeminence of the scripture over every other source of revelation or doctrine. We have already made reference to the great world-wide outpouring of the Holy Spirit in the last days and to the various supernatural manifestations which will accompany this outpouring. However, the scripture also warns us that, side by side with this increased activity and manifestation of the Holy Spirit, there will be a parallel increase in the activity of the satanic and demonic forces which always seek to oppose and strive against God's people and God's purposes in the earth.

Speaking about this same closing period of time, Christ Himself warns us, in Matthew's Gospel, chapter 24, verses 23, 24 and 25: "Then if any man shall say unto you, Lo, here is Christ, or there; believe it not. For there shall arise false Christs, and false prophets, and shall show great signs and wonders; insomuch that, if it were possible, they shall deceive the very elect. Behold, I have told you before."

In the same way, the apostle Paul warns us in First Timothy, chapter 4, verses 1, 2 and 3: "Now the Spirit speaketh expressly, that in the latter times some shall depart from the faith, giving heed to seducing spirits, and doctrines of devils (or demons); speaking lies in hyprocrisy...forbidding to marry, and commanding to abstain from meats, which God hath created to be received with thanksgiving of them which believe and know the truth." Paul here warns us that in these days there will be a great increase in the propagation of false doctrines and cults, and that the unseen cause behind this will be the activity of seducing spirits and demons. As examples, he mentions religious doctrines and practices which impose unnatural and unscriptural forms of asceticism in regard to diet and to the normal marriage relationship. Paul indicates that the safeguard against being deceived by these forms of religious error is to "believe and know the truth"--that is, the truth of God's Word. By this divine standard of truth we are enabled to detect and to reject all forms of satanic error and deception. But for the people who profess religion, without sound faith and knowledge of what the scripture teaches, these are indeed perilous days.

* * *

We need to lay hold upon one great guiding principle which is established in the scripture. It is this: God's Word and God's Spirit should always work together in perfect unity and harmony. We should never divorce the Word from the Spirit, or the Spirit from the Word. It is not God's plan that the Word should ever work apart from the Spirit, or the Spirit apart from the Word.

In Psalm 33, verse 6, we read: "By the word of the Lord were the heavens made; and all the host of them by the breath of his mouth." The word here translated "breath" is actually the normal Hebrew word for "spirit." However, the use of the word "breath" suggests a beautiful picture of the working of God's Spirit. As God's Word goes out of His mouth, so His Spirit--which is His breath--goes with it.

On our human level, it is a fact that each time we open our mouths to speak a word, our breath necessarily goes out together with the word. So it is also with God. As God's Word goes forth, His breath--that is, His Spirit--goes with it. In this way, God's Word and God's Spirit are always together, perfectly united in one single divine operation.

We see this fact illustrated, as the Psalmist reminds us, in the account of creation. In Genesis chapter 1, verse 2, we read: "The Spirit of God moved upon the face of the waters." In the next verse we read: "And God said, Let there be light; and there was light." That is, God's Word went forth, God pronounced the word "Light." And as the Word and the Spirit of God were thus united, creation took place, light came into being, God's purpose was fulfilled.

What was true of that great act of creation is true also of the life of each individual. God's Word and God's Spirit united in our lives contain all the creative authority and power of God Himself. Through them God will supply every need and will work out His perfect will and plan for us. But if we divorce these two from one another--seeking the Spirit without the Word, or studying the Word apart from the Spirit--we go astray and miss God's plan.

To seek the manifestations of the Spirit apart from the Word will always end in foolishness, fanaticism, and error. To profess the Word without the quickening of the Spirit, results only in dead, powerless orthodoxy and religious formalism.

* * *

In closing, let me summarize briefly the main conclusions of our present study:

We build upon the foundation of Christ in our lives by hearing and doing the Word of God. Thus, it is God's Word which builds us up.

God's Word is the test of our discipleship and of our love for God; it is the way by which Christ manifests Himself to us, and by which God in His fulness comes to make His abode with us.

As we move forward in the grea last day outpouring of God's Spirit which is now taking place, we need, more than ever before, to hold fast to God's Word.

God's Word and God's Spirit united in our lives will

accomplish God's perfect will for us.

* * *

In our next study in this series, we shall consider the authority of God's Word.

III
The Authority of God's Word

*The Bible - God's Written Word - Eternal - Authoritative -
Inspired By The Holy Ghost*

Welcome to the Study Hour.

Our textbook–the Bible.

Again today we present to you the Bible's own challenge:
Study for yourself! "Taste and see!" Don't argue or reject,
until you have found out for yourself what the Bible really
teaches. Don't be content with second-hand opinions or traditions. Find out for yourself. You will find that the effort
required to do this will be repaid many times over by the
results achieved.

Stay with us now as we continue to examine this important
subject, "Foundations."

In our two previous studies in this series we have reached
the following conclusions:

First, the only foundation of all true Christian faith is none
other than Christ Himself–Christ encountered, Christ revealed,
Christ acknowledged, Christ confessed.

Second, we build upon this foundation of Christ in our
lives by hearing and doing the Word of God–by studying
and applying the Bible. It is the Bible that builds us up.
It is through the Bible, the written Word of God, that Christ
Himself, the living Word, the Word made flesh, comes into
our lives.

Thus our attitude to the Bible is the proof of our discipleship; the test of our love for Christ; the way by which Christ
reveals Himself to us.

Because of the unique and supreme importance of the
Bible in the Christian life, we shall now examine in some detail
what the Bible actually has to say about itself–the claims which
it makes on its own behalf. Mainly, we shall consider two
particular claims which the Bible makes–the authority which it
claims to possess, and the effects which it claims to produce.

* * *

In our study today we shall discuss the authority of the
Bible.

We do well to commence our study of this subject by turning to the words of Christ Himself, recorded in John's Gospel, chapter 10, verses 34, 35 and 36. Christ is here speaking to the Jews, and He is justifying the claim which He has made, and which the Jews had contested, that He is the Son of God. In support of His claim, Christ quotes from the Book of Psalms in the Old Testament, which he designates by the phrase, "your law." Here is what He says:

"Jesus answered them, Is it not written in your law, I said, Ye are gods?

"If he called them gods, unto whom the Word of God came, and the scripture cannot be broken;

"Say ye of him, whom the Father hath sanctified, and sent into the world, Thou blasphemest; because I said, I am the Son of God?"

In this reply Jesus Himself makes use of the two titles which have ever since been used more than all others by His followers to designate the Bible. The first of these titles is "the Word of God"; the second is "the Scripture." It will be profitable to consider what each of these two main titles has to tell us about the nature of the Bible.

When Jesus called the Bible "the Word of God," He indicated that the truths revealed in it did not have their origin with men, but with God. Though many different men have been used in various ways to make the Bible available to the world, they are all merely instruments or channels. In no case did the message or the revelation of the Bible originate with men, but always and only with God Himself.

On the other hand, when Jesus used the second title—"the Scripture"—He indicated a divinely appointed limitation of the Bible. The phrase "the Scripture" means literally "that which is written." The Bible does not contain the entire knowledge or purpose of Almighty God in every aspect or detail. It does not even contain all the divinely inspired messages that God has ever given through human instruments. This is proved by the fact that the Bible itself refers in many places to the utterances of prophets whose words are not recorded in the Bible. We see, therefore, that the Bible, though completely true and authoritative, is also highly selective. Its message is intended primarily for the human race. It is expressed in words and in terms which human beings can understand. Its central theme and purpose is the spiritual welfare of man. It reveals primarily the nature and consequences of sin, and the way of deliverance from sin and its consequences through faith in Christ.

Let us now take one more brief look at the words of Jesus in John chapter 10, verse 35. Not merely does He here set His personal seal of approval upon the Bible's two main titles--"the Word of God," and "the Scripture." He also sets His seal of approval quite clearly upon the Bible's claim to complete authority, for He says, "...and the scripture cannot be broken." This short phrase, "cannot be broken," contains within it every claim for supreme and divine authority that can ever be made on behalf of the Bible. Volumes of controversy may be written either for or against the Bible, but in the last resort Jesus has said all that is necessary in five short, simple words--"The Scripture cannot be broken."

* * *

When we give proper weight to the Bible's claim that the men associated with it were in every case merely instruments or channels, and that every message and revelation in it has its origin with God Himself, there remains no logical or reasonable ground for rejecting the Bible's claim to complete authority. We are living in days when men can launch satellites into space, and then by means of invisible forces such as radio, radar, or electronics, control the course of these satellites at distances of thousands or millions of miles, can maintain communication with them, and can receive communication from them. If men can achieve such results as these, then only blind prejudice--and that of a most unscientific character--would deny the possibility that God could create human beings with mental and spiritual faculties such that He could control or direct them, maintain communication with them, and receive communication from them. The Bible asserts that this is, in fact, what God has done, and still continues to do. The discoveries and inventions of modern science, so far from discrediting the claims of the Bible, make it easier for honest and open-minded people to picture the kind of relationship between God and men which made the Bible possible.

The Bible indicates plainly tht there was one supreme, invisible influence by which God did in fact control, direct and communicate with the spirits and minds of the men by whom the Bible was written. This invisible influence is the Holy

Spirit—God's own Spirit.

For example, in Second Timothy, chapter 3, verse 16, the apostle Paul says: "**All** scripture is given by **inspiration of God**, and is profitable for doctrine, for reproof, for correction, for instruction in righteousness." The Word here translated "by inspiration" means literally "inbreathed of God," and is directly connected with the word "Spirit." In other words, the Spirit of God—the Holy Spirit—was the invisible, but inerrant, influence which controlled and directed all those who wrote the various parts of the Bible.

This is stated perhaps more plainly still by the apostle Peter, in his Second Epistle, Chapter 1, verses 20 and 21.

First of all, he says in verse 20: "Knowing this first, that no prophecy of the scripture is of any private interpretation." In other words, as we have already explained, in no case does the message or revelationof the Bible originate with man, but always with God.

Then in verse 21 Peter goes on to explain just how this took place: "For the prophecy came not in old time by the will of man; but holy men of God spake as they were moved by the Holy Ghost." The Greek word here translated "moved by" means more literally "borne along by," or we might say "directed in their course by." In other words, just as men today control the course of their satellites in space by the interplay of radio and electronics, so God controlled the men who wrote the Bible by the interplay of His divine Spirit with the spiritual and mental faculties of man. In the face of contemporary scientific evidence, to deny the possibility of God doing this is merely to give expression to prejudice.

In the Old Testament the same truth of divine inspiration is presented to us in another picture, taken from an activity which goes much further back into human history than the contemporary launching of satellites into space. In Psalm 12, verse 6, the Psalmist David says: "The words of the Lord are pure words: as silver tried in a furnace of earth, purified seven times." The picture is taken from the process of purifying silver in a furnace, or oven, built of clay (such clay ovens are still used for various purposes among the Arabs today.) The application of this picture to the writing of the Bible is as follows. The clay furnace represents the human element. The silver represents the divine message which is to be conveyed through the human channel. The fire which ensures the absolute purity of the silver, that is, the absolute accuracy of the message, represents the Holy Spirit. The phrase "seven times" indicates--as the number seven does in many passages of the Bible--the absolute perfection of the Holy Spirit's work. Thus, the whole picture assures us that the complete accuracy of the divine message in the scriptures is due to the perfect operation of the Holy Spirit, overruling all the frailty of human clay, and purging all the dross of human error from the flawless silver of God's message to man.

* * *

Probably no character in the Old Testament had a clearer understanding than the Psalmist David of the truth and authority of God's Word. In Psalm 119, verse 89, he says: "For ever, O Lord, thy word is settled in heaven." Here David emphasizes that the Bible is not the product of time, but of eternity. It contains the eternal mind and counsel of God formed before the beginning of time or the foundation of the world. Out of eternity it has been projected through human channels into this world of time, but when time and the world shall have passed away, the mind and counsel of God revealed through the scriptures will still stand unmoved and unchanged. The same thought is expressed by Christ Himself in Matthew's Gospel, chapter 24, verse 35, where He says: "Heaven and earth shall pass away, but my words shall not pass away."

Again in Psalm 119, verse 160, David says: "Thy word is true from the beginning." Now in the Hebrew scriptures the title of the first book of the Bible, the book of Genesis, is taken from the opening phrase of the book, "In the beginning..." Right up to the present day, the Hebrew title of the book, which we know as Genesis, is "In the beginning." Therefore, when David says, "Thy word is true from the beginning," he is specially referring to the book of Genesis. In the last century or two, persistent criticism and attack have been directed against almost every part of the Bible, both Old and New Testaments. However, by far the greatest part of this attack has always been focused on the book of Genesis and the next four books which follow it; that is, on the first five books of the Bible, known as the Pentateuch, and attributed to the authorship of Moses. It is remarkable, therefore, that nearly three thousand years before these attacks against the Pentateuch were conceived in the minds of men, David had already given the Holy Spirit's testimony to the faith of God's believing people throughout all ages: "Thy word is true from the beginning." In other words, the Bible is true from Genesis, chapter 1, verse 1, and right on through.

Certainly, if we are willing to give words their plain and obvious meaning, there can be no question that Christ and His apostles, like all believing Jews of their time, accepted the absolute truth and authority of all the Old Testament scriptures, including the five books of the Pentateuch.

In the account of Christ's temptation by Satan in the wilderness, recorded in Matthew's Gospel, chapter 4, verses 1 through 10, we read that Christ answered each temptation of Satan by direct quotation from the Old Testament scriptures. Three times He commenced His answer with the phrase, "It is written..." Each time he was quoting directly from the fifth book of the Pentateuch, the book of Deuteronomy. It is a remarkable fact that not only Christ, but also Satan, accepted the absolute authority of this book.

In the Sermon on the Mount, in Matthew, chapter 5, verses 17 and 18, Christ said: "Think not that I am come to destroy the law, or the prophets" (This phrase "the law and the prophets" was generally used to designate the Old Testament scriptures as a whole): "I am not come to destroy, but to fulfil. For verily I say unto you, Till heaven and earth pass, one jot or one tittle shall in no wise pass from the law, till all be fulfilled." (The phrase "the law" was used to designate primarily the five books of Moses--that is, the Pentateuch--but also, by extension, the rest of the Old Testament.)

The word "jot" is the English form of the name of the smallest letter in the Hebrew alphabet, roughly corresponding in size and shape to an inverted comma in modern English script. The word "tittle" indicates a little curl, or horn--smaller in size than a comma--added at the corner of certain letters in the Hebrew alphabet to distinguish them from other letters very similar in shape. Thus what Christ here says in effect is that the original text of the Hebrew scriptures is so accurate and authoritative that not even one portion of the script smaller in size than a comma can be altered or removed. It is scarcely possible to conceive how Christ could have used any form of speech which would have more thoroughly endorsed the absolute accuracy and authority of the Old Testament scriptures.

Consistently throughout His earthly teaching ministry He maintained the same attitude toward the Old Testament scriptures. For instance, we read in Matthew, chapter 19, verses 3 through 9, that when the Pharisees raised a question about marriage and divorce, Christ answered by referring them to the account of the creation given in the opening chapters of Genesis. He introduced His answer by the question, "Have ye not read that he which made them at the beginning made them male and female?" Notice once again that the phrase "at the beginning" constituted a direct reference to the book of Genesis.

Again, when the Sadducees raised a question about the resurrection from the dead, we read in Matthew chapter 22, verses 31 and 32, that Christ answered them by referring to the account of Moses at the burning bush given in the second book of the Pentateuch, the book of Exodus. As with the Pharisees, so with the Sadducees, Christ expressed His reply in the form of a question: "Have ye not read that which was spoken unto you by God, saying, I am the God of Abraham, and the God of Isaac, and the God of Jacob?" Christ here quotes from the book of Exodus, chapter 3, verse 6. But in quoting these words recorded by Moses nearly fifteen centuries earlier, Christ said to the Sadducees of His own day, "Have ye not read that which was **spoken unto you by God?**" Note that phrase "spoken unto you by God." In other words, Christ did not regard these writings of Moses as merely a historical document of the past, but rather as a living, up-to-date, authoritative message direct from God to the people of His own day. The passage of fifteen centuries had not deprived the record of Moses of its vitality, its accuracy, or its authority.

Not merely did Christ accept the absolute accuracy of the Old Testament scriptures in all His teaching; he also acknowledged their absolute authority and control over the whole course of His own earthly life. From His birth to His death and resurrection, there was one supreme controlling principle, which was expressed in the phrase, "that it might be fulfilled." That which was to be fulfilled was in every case some relevant scripture of the Old Testament. By way of illustration, we may mention the following incidents in the earthly life of Jesus, concerning each of which it was specifically recorded that they took place in fulfilment of Old Testament scriptures:

His birth of a virgin; His birth at Bethlehem; His flight into Egypt; His dwelling at Nazareth; His being anointed by the Holy Spirit; His ministry in Galilee; His healing of the sick; the rejection of His teaching and His miracles by the Jews; His use of parables; His being betrayed by a friend; His being forsaken by His disciples; His being hated without a cause; His being condemned with criminals; His garments being parted and divided by lot; His being offered vinegar for His thirst; His body being pierced without His bones being broken; His being buried in a rich man's tomb; His rising from the dead on the third day.

This list, which is by no means exhaustive, contains eighteen incidents in the earthly life of Jesus, concerning every one of which it is specifically recorded that they took place in order that the scriptures of the Old Testament might be fulfilled. It is therefore possible to say, without exaggeration or misrepresentation, that the entire earthly life of Jesus, from His birth to His resurrection, was controlled and directed in every aspect and in every stage by the absolute authority of the Old Testament scriptures.

When we set this fact side by side with His own unquestioning acceptance of the Old Testament scriptures in all His teaching, we are left with only one possible or logical conclusion: If the Old Testament scriptures are not an absolutely accurate and authoritative revelation from God, then Jesus Christ Himself was either deceived, or He was a deceiver.

* * *

Let us now turn from the Old Testament to the New, and let us consider the authority claimed for the New Testament.

We must first observe the remarkable fact that, so far as we know, Christ Himself never set down a single word in writing--with the exception of one occasion when He wrote on the ground in the presence of a woman taken in adultery.

Nevertheless, Christ explicitly commanded His disciples to transmit the record of His ministry and His preaching to all nations of the earth, for in Matthew chapter 28, verses 19 and 20, he said to them: "Go ye therefore, and teach--or make disciples of--all nations...teaching them to observe all things whatsoever I have commanded you." Again in Matthew chapter 23, verse 34, He said: "Behold I send unto you prophets, and wise men, and scribes..."The word "scribes" means "writers"; that is, those who set down religious teaching in written form. It is therefore clear that Jesus intended the record of His ministry and teaching to be set down by His disciples in permanent form.

Furthermore, Jesus made all necessary provisions for the absolute accuracy of all that He intended His disciples to put down in writing, for He promised to send the Holy Spirit to them for this very purpose. In John's Gospel, chapter 14, verse 26, He says: "But the Comforter, which is the Holy Ghost, whom the Father will send in my name, he shall teach you all things, and bring all things to your remembrance, whatsoever I have said unto you." A further, similar promise is contained in John chapter 16, verses 13 through 15.

Notice that in these words Christ made provision both for past and for future; that is, both for the accurate recording of those things which the disciples had already seen and heard, and also for the accurate imparting of the new truths which the Holy Spirit would thereafter reveal to them. The past is pro-provided for in the phrase, "He shall bring all things to your remembrance, whatsoever I have said unto you." The future is provided for in the phrase, "He shall teach you all things"– and again, in John 16, verse 13, "He will guide you into all truth."

We see, therefore, that the accuracy and authority of the New Testament, like that of the Old Testament, depends not upon human observation, memory or understanding, but upon the teaching, guidance and control of the Holy Spirit. For this reason, the apostle Paul says, "All scripture"-- Old Testament, and New Testament alike–"is given by inspiration of God."

We find that the apostles themselves clearly understood this and laid claim to this authority in their writings. For example, the apostle Peter, in his Second Epistle, chapter 3, verses 1 and 2, writes: "This second epistle, beloved, I now write unto you...that ye may be mindful of the words which were spoken before by the holy prophets, and of the commandment of us the apostles of the Lord and Saviour." Here Peter sets the scriptures of the Old Testament prophets and the written commandments of Christ's apostles side by side, as being of precisely equal authority. Again, in verses 15 and 16 of the same chapter, the apostle Peter acknowledges the divine authority of the writings of Paul, for he says: "And account that the longsuffering of our Lord is salvation; even as our beloved brother Paul also according to the wisdom given unto him hath written unto you; as also in all his epistles, speaking in them of these things; in which are some things hard to be understood, which they that are unlearned and unstable wrest, as they do also **the other scriptures,** unto their own destruction." These words indicate that even in the lifetime of Paul himself, the other apostles acknowledged that Paul's epistles possessed the full authority of scriptures. Yet Paul himself had never known Jesus in His earthly ministry. Therefore, the accuracy and authority of Paul's teaching depended solely upon the supernatural inspiration and revelation of the Holy Spirit.

The same applies to Luke, who never received the title of an "apostle." Nevertheless, in the preamble to his Gospel, chapter 1, verse 3, he states that he "had perfect understanding of all things from the very first." The Greek word here translated "from the very first" means literally "from above." In John chapter 3, verse 3, where Jesus speaks of "being born again," it is the same Greek word which is translated "again." In each of these passages, the word indicates the direct, supernatural intervention and operation of the Holy Spirit.

Thus we find, on careful examination, that the claim to absolute accuracy and authority of both Old and New Testaments alike depends not on the variable and fallible faculties of human beings, but on the divine, supernatural guidance, revelation and control of the Holy Spirit. Interpreted together in this way, the Old and New Testaments confirm and complement each other, and constitute a coherent, complete, and all-sufficient revelation of God.

We have also seen that there is nothing in this total view of the scriptures which is inconsistent with logic, science, or common sense. On the contrary, there is much in all three to confirm such a view and render it easy to believe.

* * *

In the studies which follow we shall go on to examine the practical effects which the Bible claims to produce in those who believe it.

IV
The Working of God's Word

Faith - The New Birth - Spiritual Nourishment

Welcome to the Study Hour.

Our textbook--The Bible.

Our study today is the fourth in the series, "Foundations."

In the three previous studies in this series, we have covered the following ground:

First, we have seen that the only foundation of all true Christian faith is none other than Christ Himself Christ encountered, Christ revealed, Christ acknowledged, Christ confessed.

Second, we have seen that we build upon the foundation of Christ in our lives by hearing and doing the Word of God--by studying and applying the Bible. It is the Bible which builds us up. It is through the Bible, the written Word of God, that Christ Himself, the Living Word, the Word made flesh, comes into our lives.

Third, we have considered the authority which the Bible claims for itself, and we have seen that the authority of all Scriptures, both Old and New Testament alike, is derived solely from one and the same source; that is, God's Holy Spirit. Though the Scriptures were produced through many different human instruments, it was the Holy Spirit which used, inspired, and controlled each and every one of these human instruments. This is summed up by the Apostle Paul in Second Timothy, chapter 3, verse 16, where he says: "All Scripture is given by inspiration of God"--or more literally, "All Scripture is inbreathed by the Spirit of God." Thus, the final authority behind all Scripture is that of the Third Person of the Godhead, the Holy Spirit Himself.

* * *

We shall now examine the practical effects which the Bible claims to produce in those who receive it.

In Hebrews, chapter 4, verse 12, we are told: "The Word of God is quick, and powerful"--or, in more modern English-- "The Word of God is alive, and active." (The Greek work translated "powerful," or "active," is the one from which we obtain the English word "energetic"). Thus, the picture conveyed to us here is one of intense, vibrant energy and activity.

Similarly, in John's Gospel, chapter 6, verse 63, Jesus Himself says: "The words that I speak unto you, they are spirit, and they are life."

Again, in First Thessalonians, chapter 2, verse 13, the Apostle Paul writes to the Christians in Thessalonica: "For this cause also thank we God without ceasing, because, when ye received the Word of God which ye heard of us, ye received it not as the word of men, but as it is in truth, the Word of God, which effectually worketh also in you that believe."

Thus, we see that God's Word cannot be reduced merely to sounds in the air or marks on a sheet of paper. On the contrary, God's Word is Life; it is Spirit; it is alive; it is active; it is energetic; it works effectually in those who believe it.

However, the Bible also makes it plain that the manner and the degree in which it works in any given instance is decided by the reaction of those who hear it. For this reason, James says in his Epistle, chapter 1, verse 21: "Wherefore lay apart all filthiness and superfluity of naughtiness, and receive with meekness the engrafted Word, which is able to save your souls." Notice that, before the Word of God can be received into the soul with saving effect, there are certain things which must be laid aside. The two things which James here specifies are "filthiness" and "naughtiness." "Filthiness" denotes a perverse delight in that which is licentious and impure. This attitude closes the mind and heart against the saving influence of God's Word. On the other hand, the word "naughtiness" particularly suggests the bad behaviour of a child. One occasion especially on which we call a child "naughty" is when it refuses to accept instruction or correction from its senior, but argues and answers back. This attitude is often found in the unregenerate soul towards God. It is referred to by the apostle Paul in Romans, chapter 9, verse 20, where he says: "Nay, but O man, who art thou that repliest against God?" It is referred to also in Job, chapter 40, verse 2, where the Lord says to Job: "Shall he that contendeth with the Almighty instruct Him? He that reproveth God, let him answer it." This attitude, like that of "filthiness," closes the heart and mind to the beneficial effects of God's Word.

On the other hand, the opposite of "filthiness" and "naughtiness" is described by James as "meekness." "Meekness" carries with it the ideas of quietness, humility, sincerity, patience, openness of heart and mind. These characteristics are in turn aften associated with what the Bible calls "the fear of the Lord"; that is, an attitude of reverence and respect towards God. Thus we read in Psalm 25, verses 8, 9, 12, and 14, the following description of the man who is able to receive benefit and blessing from the instruction of God through His Word:

"Good and upright is the Lord: therefore will He teach sinners in the way.

The **meek** will He guide in judgement: and the **meek** will He teach His way...

What man is he that **feareth the Lord?** Him shall He teach in the way that He shall choose...

The secret of the Lord is with **them that fear Him:** and He will shew them His covenant."

We see here that **meekness** and the **fear of the Lord** are the two attitudes which are necessary in those who desire to receive instruction and blessing from God through His Word. These two attitudes are the opposites of those which James describes as "filthiness" and "naughtiness."

Thus, we find that God's Word can produce quite different effects in different people, and that these effects are decided by the reactions of those who hear it. For this reason, we read in Hebrews, chapter 4, verse 12, not merely that God's Word is "alive" and "active," but also that it "is a discerner of the thoughts and intents of the heart." In other words, God's Word brings out into the open the inward nature and character of those who hear it, and distinguishes sharply between the different types of hearers.

In like manner, Paul describes the dividing and revealing character of the gospel in First Corinthians, chapter 1, verse 18: "For the preaching of the cross is to them that perish foolishness; but unto us which are saved it is the power of God." There is no difference in the message preached; the message is the same to all men. The difference lies in the reaction of those who hear. For those who react in one way, the message appears to be mere foolishness; for those who react in the opposite way, the message becomes the saving power of God actually experienced in their lives.

This leads us to yet another fact about the Word of God which is stated in that key verse, Hebrews chapter 4, verse 12. Not only is the Word of God "alive" and "active"; not only is it a discerner, or revealer, of the thoughts and intents of the heart; it is also **"sharper than any two-edged sword."** That is, it divides all those who hear into two classes-- those who reject and call it foolishness, and those who receive and find in it the saving power of God.

It was in this sense that Christ said, in Matthew chapter 10, verse 34: "Think not that I am come to send peach on earth; I came not to send peace, but a sword. For I am come to set a man at variance against his father, and the daughter against her mother, and the daughter-in-law against her mother-in-law." The sword which Christ came to send upon earth is that which John saw, in Revelation chapter 1, verse 16, proceeding out of Christ's mouth--the sharp two-edged sword of God's Word. This sword, as it goes forth through the earth, divides even between members of the same household, severing the closest of earthly bonds, according as each member of the household reacts toward it.

* * *

Turning now to those who receive God's Word with meekness and sincerity, with openness of heart and mind, let us examine in order the various effects which it produces.

The first of these effects is: **Faith.** This is stated in Romans chapter 10, verse 17: "So then faith cometh by hearing, and hearing by the Word of God."

Notice that there are three successive stages in the spiritual process here described. First, God's Word; second, hearing; third, faith. God's Word does not immediately produce faith, but only "hearing." Hearing may be described as an attitude of aroused interest and attention, a sincere desire to receive and to understand the message presented. Then out of "hearing" there develops faith. It is most important to see that the hearing of God's Word initiates a process in the soul, out of which faith develops, and that this process requires a certain minimum period of time. This explains why there is so little faith to be found among so many professing Christians today. The reason is that they never devote enough time to the hearing of God's Word to allow it to produce in them any substantial proportion of faith. If they ever devote any time at all to private devotions and the study of God's Word, the whole thing is conducted in such a hurried and haphazard way that it is all over before faith has had time to develop. Those who wish to develop real personal faith within their soul must be prepared to devote ample time to the unhurried hearing of God's Word.

As we study how faith is produced, we also come to understand much more clearly how scriptural faith should be defined. In general conversation, we use the word "faith" very freely. We speak of having faith in a doctor, or faith in a medicine, or faith in a newspaper, or faith in a politician, or a political party. In scriptural terms, however, the word "faith" must be much more strictly defined. Since faith comes only from hearing God's Word, faith is always directly related to God's Word. Scriptural faith does not consist in believing anything that we ourselves may wish or please or fancy. Scriptural faith may be defined as believing that God means what He has said in His Word--or again, as believing that God will do what He has promised in His Word to do.

For example, we see that David exercised this scriptural kind of faith in First Chronicles chapter 17, verse 23, when he said to the Lord: "Therefore now, Lord, let the thing that thou hast spoken concerning thy servant and concerning his house be established forever, and do as thou hast said." Scriptural faith is expressed in those five short words: "do as thou hast said."

Likewise, the virgin Mary exercised the same kind of scriptural faith, when the angel Gabriel brought her a message of promise from God, and she replied, in Luke's Gospel, chapter 1, verse 38: "Be it unto me according to thy word." That is the secret of scriptural fiath-"according to thy word." Scriptural faith is produced within the soul by the hearing of God's Word, and then is expressed by the active response of claiming the fulfilment of that which God has said.

We have emphasized that faith is the first effect produced in the soul by God's Word, because faith of this kind is basic to any positive transaction between God and any human soul. This is expressed in Hebrews chapter 11, verse 6: "But without faith it is impossible to please him; for he that cometh to God must believe that he is, and that he is a rewarder of them that diligently seek him." "He that cometh to God must believe." We see that faith is the first and indispensable response of the human soul in its approach to God.

* * *

After faith, the next great effect produced by God's Word within the soul is that spiritual experience which is called in scripture "the new birth," or "being born again." Thus James says in his Epistle, chapter 1, verse 18, that God "of his own will begat us with the word of truth, that we should be a kind of firstfruits of his creatures." The born-again Christian possesses a new kind of spiritual life begotten within him by the Word of God received by faith in his soul.

Similarly, the apostle Peter in his First Epistle, chapter 1, verse 23, describes Christians as "being born again, not of corruptible seed, but of incorruptible, by the word of God, which liveth and abideth forever." It is a principle, both in nature and in scripture, that the type of seed determines the type of life which is produced from the seed. A seed of corn produces corn; a seed of barley produces barley; an orange seed produces an orange. So it is also in the new birth. The seed is the divine, incorruptible, eternal Word of God. The life which this seed produces, when received by faith into the heart of the believer, is like the seed--it is divine, incorruptible, eternal--it is in fact the very life of God Himself coming into a human soul through His Word.

For this reason the apostle John writes in his First Epistle, chapter 3, verse 9: "Whosoever is born of God doth not commit sin, for his seed remaineth in him: and he cannot sin, because he is born of God." The apostle John here directly relates the victorious life of the overcoming Christian to the nature of the seed which produced that life within him--that is, God's own seed--the incorruptible seed of God's Word. Because the seed is incorruptible, the life which it produces is also incorruptible, that is, absolutely pure and holy.

However, it is necessary to warn that this scripture does not assert that a born-again Christian can never commit sin. Within every born-again Christian, a completely new nature has come into being. This new nature is called by Paul, in Ephesians chapter 4, verses 22 to 24, "the new man," and it is there contrasted with "the old man"; that is, with the old, corrupt, depraved, fallen nature which dominates every person who has never been born again. There is a complete and total contrast between these two: the "new man" is righteous and holy; the "old man" is depraved and corrupt. The "new man", being born of God, cannot commit sin; the "old man," being the product of man's rebellion and fall, cannot help committing sin.

The kind of life which any born-again Christian leads is the outcome of the interplay within him of these two natures, the "new man" and the "old man." So long as the "old man" is kept in subjection and the "new man" exercises his proper control, there is unsullied righteousness, victory and peace. But whenever the "old man" is allowed to reassert himself and regain his control, then the inevitable consequence is failure, defeat, and sin.

We sum up the contrast in this way: The true Christian, who has been born again of the incorruptible seed of God's Word, has within himself the possibility of leading a life of complete victory over sin. The unregenerate man, who has never been born again, has no alternative but to commit sin. He is inevitably the slave of his own corrupt, fallen nature.

* * *

We have said that the new birth through God's Word produces within the soul a completely new nature--a completely new kind of life. This leads us naturally to consider the next main effect which God's Word produces. In every realm of life, there is one unchanging law: as soon as a new life is born, the first and greatest need of that new life is suitable nourishment to sustain it. For example, when a human baby is born, that baby may be sound and healthy in every respect, but unless it quickly receives the kind of nourishment its nature demands, it will pine away and die.

The same is true in the spiritual realm. When a person is born again, the new spiritual nature produced within that person immediately requires suitable spiritual nourishment, both to maintain life and to promote growth. The spiritual nourishment which God has provided for all His born-again children is found in His own Word. God's Word is so rich and varied that it contains nourishment adapted to every stage of spiritual development.

God's provision for the first stages of spiritual growth is described in the First Epistle of Peter. Immediately after Peter has spoken, in chapter 1, about being born again of the incorruptible seed of God's Word, Peter goes on to say in chapter 2, verses 1 and 2: "Wherefore laying aside all malice, and all guile, and hypocrisies, and envies, and all evil speakings, as newborn babes, desire **the sincere milk of the word**, that ye may grow thereby." We see here that for newborn spiritual babes in Christ, God's appointed nourishment is the sincere or pure milk of His own Word, and that this milk is a necessary condition of continued life and growth.

However, there is a warning attached here. In the natural order, no matter how pure and fresh milk may be, it easily becomes contaminated and spoiled if it is brought into contact with anything that is sour and rancid. The same is true spiritually. For newborn Christians to receive proper nourishment from the pure milk of God's Word, their hearts must first be thoroughly cleansed from all that is sour or rancid. For this reason the apostle Peter warns us that we must "lay aside all **malice**, and all **guile**, and **hypocrisies**, and **envies**, and all **evil speakings**." These are the sour and rancid elements of the old life which, if they are not purged from our hearts, will frustrate the beneficial effects of God's Word within us and will hinder spiritual health and growth.

However, it is not the will of God that Christians should

continue in spiritual infancy too long. As they begin to grow up, God's Word offers them more substantial food. In Matthew's Gospel, chapter 4, verse 4, we read that when Christ was tempted by Satan to turn stones into bread, He replied: "It is written, Man shall not live by bread alone, but **by every word that proceedeth out of the mouth of God.**" Christ here indicates that God's Word is the spiritual counterpart of bread in man's natural diet. In other words, it is the main basic item of diet and source of strength.

It is significant that Christ said here with emphasis, "**every word** that proceedeth out of the mouth of God." In other words, Christians who wish to mature spiritually must learn to study the whole Bible, not just a few of the more familiar portions. It is said of George Mueller that he regularly read his whole Bible through several times each year. This explains in large measure the triumphs of his faith and the fruitfulness of his ministry. Yet there are many professing Christians and church members who scarcely know where to find in their Bibles such books as Ezra and Nehemiah, or some of the minor prophets. Far less have they ever studied for themselves the messages of such books as these. No wonder that they continue forever in a kind of spiritual infancy. They are, in fact, sad examples of retarded development due to inadequate diet.

Beyond milk and bread, God's Word also provides "strong meat." This is described in Hebrews, chapter 5, verses 12 through 14. The writer of Hebrews here rebukes the Hebrew Christians of his day on the ground that they had been familiar for many years with the scriptures, but had never learned to make any proper study or application of their teaching, and that consequently they were still spiritually immature and unable to help others who stood in need of spiritual teaching. This is what the writer says: "For when for the time ye ought to be teachers, ye have need that one teach you again which be the first principles--or elements--of the oracles of God; and are become such as have need of milk, and not of strong meat.

"For every one that useth milk is unskilful-or inexperienced-in the word of righteousness: for he is a babe.

"But **strong meat** belongeth to them that are of full age-or mature--even those who by reason of use have their senses exercised to discern both good and evil."

What a picture of a great mass of professing Christians and church members today! They have owned a Bible and attended church for many years. Yet how little they know of what the Bible teaches! How weak and immature they are in their own spiritual experience; how little able to counsel a sinner or instruct a new convert! After so many years, still spiritual babes, unable to digest any kind of teaching that goes beyond milk!

However, it is not necessary to remain in this condition. Th writer of Hebrews tells us the remedy. It is to "have our senses exercised by reason of use," that is, to develop our spiritual faculties by regular, systematic study of the whole of God's Word.

* * *

With this appropriate word of exhortation from Hebrews, we must close our study today. We have spoken of three main effects of God's Word: faith, the new birth, and spiritual nourishment.

In the studies which follow we shall go on to examine several other effects of great importance which God's Word produces in the believer.

V
The Working of God's Word

Physical Healing - Mental Illumination

Welcome to the Study Hour.

Our textbook--the Bible.

Stay with us now for the fifth study in our present series, "Foundations."

In the previous studies in this series, we have examined the basic foundation of the Christian faith.

We have seen that this foundation is none other than Christ Himself--Christ encountered, Christ revealed, Christ acknowledged, Christ confessed.

We have seen that, once this foundation of Christ has been laid in our lives, thereafter we build upon it by studying and applying the Bible; and that it is through the Bible, studied and applied, that Christ manifests Himself to us and comes in to us to take full possession and control of our lives.

Because of the supremely important place of the Bible in the Christian life, we have examined the authority which it claims for itself as the Word of God; and we have seen that, though many human instruments were used to make the Bible available as God's Word to man, the supreme authority behind them all is that of the Holy Spirit--the Third Person of the Godhead.

Finally, we have commenced to examine the various effects which the Bible, as God's Word, produces in the lives of those who receive it with openness of heart and mind, and up to this point we have discovered the following three effects:

First, God's Word produces **faith**; and faith in turn is directly related to God's Word, because faith consists in believing and acting upon what God has said in His Word.

Second, God's Word, received as incorruptible seed into a believer's heart, produces the **new birth**, that is, a completely new spiritual nature created within the believer, and called in the scriptures "the new man."

Third, God's Word is the divinely appointed **spiritual nourishment** with which the believer must regularly feed the new nature within him, if he is to grow into a healthy, strong, mature Christian.

We shall now see that God's Word is so varied and wonderful in its working that it provides not merely **spiritual** health and strength for the soul, but also **physical** health and strength for the **body.**

For our first text in this connection, let us turn to Psalm 107, verses 17 through 20: "Fools, because of their transgression, and because of their iniquities, are afflicted. Their soul abhorreth all manner of meat; and they draw near unto the gates of death. Then they cry unto the Lord in their trouble, and He saveth them out of their distresses. **He sent his word, and healed them** and delivered them from their destructions."

The Psalmist here gives us a picture of men so desperately sick that they have lost all appetite for food, and they are lying right at death's door. In their extremity they cry unto the Lord, and He sends them that which they cry for--healing and deliverance. By what means does He send these? By nothing else but by His own Word. For the Psalmist says: "He sent his word, and healed them, and delivered them from their destructions." We see, therefore, that both healing and deliverance are sent to us through God's Word.

Side by side with this passage in Psalm 107 we may set the passage in Isaiah chapter 55, verse 11, where God says: "So shall my word be that goeth forth out of my mouth: it shall not return unto me void, but it shall accomplish that which I please, and it shall prosper in the thing whereto I sent it."

In Psalm 107, verse 20, we read that God sent His Word to heal and to deliver; and in Isaiah chapter 55, verse 11, God says that His Word will accomplish and will prosper in the thing whereto He sent it. Thus God absolutely guarantees to provide healing through His Word.

This truth of physical healing through God's Word is even more fully stated in the Book of Proverbs, chapter 4, verses 20-22, where God says: "My son, attend to my words; incline thine ear unto my sayings. Let them not depart from thine eyes; keep them in the midst of thine heart. For they are life unto those that find them, **and health to all their flesh.**" What promise of physical healing could be more all-inclusive than that: **health to all their flesh**"? Every part of our entire physical frame is included in this phrase. There is nothing omitted. Furthermore, in the margin of the standard King James Version, the alternative reading for "health" is "medicine." The same Hebrew word includes both shades of meaning. Thus God has here committed Himself to providing complete physical healing and health.

Notice the introductory phrase at the beginning of verse 20: "My son." This indicates that God is here speaking to His own believing children. In Matthew's Gospel, chapter 15, verse 26, we read that a Syro-Phoenician woman came to Christ to plead for the healing of her daughter, and that Christ replied to her request by saying, "It is not meet to take the children's bread, and to cast it to dogs." By these words Christ indicated that healing is "the children's bread"; in other words, it is part of God's appointed daily portion for all His children. It is not a luxury for which they have to make special pleas, and which may or may not be granted them. No, it is their "bread"--it is part of their basic, appointed daily provision from their heavenly Father. This agrees exactly with the passage which we have read in Proverbs, chapter 4, where God's promise of perfect healing and health is addressed to one of God's believing children.

Notice also that here in Proverbs, chapter 4, as in Psalm 107, the means by which God provides healing is through His own Word, for He says: "My Son, attend to my words; incline thine ear unto my sayings. For they-- that is, my words, my sayings--they are life to those that find them, and health to all their flesh." The divine life of God Himself, sufficient for every need of soul and body alike, is in His Word and is freely imparted to those who receive His Word by faith. This is one further example of the vital truth which we stressed earlier in this series, that God Himself is in His Word, and that it is through His Word that He comes into our lives.

* * *

As we consider the claim made here in Proverbs 4, verses 20-22, that God's Words are medicine for all our flesh, we might quite justifiably call these three verses God's great "medicine bottle," containing a medicine such as was never compounded on earth, one medicine guaranteed to cure all diseases. However, we must bear in mind that on the human level, when the doctor prescribes a medicine, he normally ensures that the directions for taking it are written clearly on the bottle, and he indicates thereby that no cure can be expected unless the medicine is taken regularly, according to the directions. The same is true with God's "medicine" here in Proverbs. The directions are "on the bottle," and no cure is guaranteed if the directions are not followed.

What are these directions? They are fourfold: First, "attend to my words"; second, "incline thine ear"; third, "let them not depart from thine eyes"; fourth, "keep them in the midst of thine heart."

Let us analyze these directions a little more closely. The first direction is, "Attend to my words." As we read God's Word, we need to give it close and careful attention. We need to focus our understanding upon it. We need to give it free, unhindered access to our whole inward being. So often we read God's Word with divided attention. Half our mind is occupied with what we read; the other half is occupied with those things which Jesus called "the cares of this life." We read some verses, or perhaps even a chapter or two, but at the end we have scarcely any clear impression or recollection of that which we have read. Our attention has wandered. Taken in this way, God's Word will not produce the effects which God intended. When reading the Bible, it is well to do what Jesus recommended when He spoke of prayer; that is, to enter our closet and shut the door. In other words, we must shut ourselves in with God and shut out the things of the world and of time.

The second direction God's "medicine bottle" is, "Incline thine ear." The inclined ear indicates humility. It is the opposite of being proud and stiff-necked. We must be teachable. We must be willing to let God teach us. In Psalm 78, verse 41, the Psalmist speaks of Israel's conduct as they wandered through the wilderness from Egypt to Canaan, and he brings this charge against them: "They limited the Holy One of Israel." In other words, by their stubbornness and unbelief they set limits to what they would allow God to do for them. Many professing Christians do just the same today. They do not approach the Bible with an open mind or a teachable spirit. They are full of prejudices or preconceptions--very often instilled by the particular sect or denomination with which they are associated--and they are not willing to accept any revelation or teaching from the scriptures which goes beyond, or contrary to, their own set thoughts. Jesus charged the religious leaders of His day with this fault, when He said, in Matthew's Gospel, chapter 15, verses 6 and 9: "Ye have made the commandment of God of none effect by your tradition...But in vain do they worship me, teaching for doctrines the commandments of men." The apostle Paul had been a prisoner of religious prejudices and traditions, but through the revelation of Christ on the Damascus road he had been set free from them, and thereafter we find him saying, in Romans chapter 3, verse 4, "Let God be true, but every man a liar." If we wish to receive the full benefit of God's Word, we must learn to take the same attitude.

The third direction on God's medicine bottle is: "Let them not depart from thine eyes"–where the word "them" refers to God's words and sayings. We may perhaps bring out the meaning of this third direction by quoting a remark of the late evangelist, Smith Wigglesworth, who once said: "The trouble with many Christians is that they have a spiritual squint: with one eye they are looking at the promises of the Lord, and with the other eye they are looking in some other direction." In order to receive the benefits of physical healing promised in God's Word, it is necessary to keep both eyes fixed unwaveringly on the Lord's promises. One mistake which many Christians make is to look away from God's promises to the case of some other Christian who has failed to receive healing. As they do this, their own faith wavers and they too fail to receive healing; for James says in his Epistle, chapter 1, verses 6, 7 and 8: "He that wavereth is like a wave of the sea driven with the wind and tossed. For let not that man think that he shall receive anything of the Lord. A double minded man is unstable in all his ways."

A helpful verse to remember in such a situation as this is is Deuteronomy, chapter 29, verse 29: "The secret things belong unto the Lord our God: but those things which are revealed belong unto us and to our children forever, that we may do all the words of this law." The reason why some Christians fail to receive healing very often remains a secret, known only to God, and not revealed to man. We do not need to be concerned with such secrets as this. Rather, we need to concern ourselves with those things which are revealed; that is, with the clear and definite statements and promises of God given to us in His Word. The things thus revealed in God's Word belong unto us and to our children forever; they are our heritage, as believers; they are our inalienable right. And they belong unto us "that we may do them"; that is, that we may act upon them in faith. When we do act upon them in this way, we prove them true in our experience.

This need of focused spiritual eyesight is referred to also by Christ Himself. One remarkable feature of human eyesight is that, although we have two separate eyes, we are able to focus them in such a way that we form one single image. This ability to focus is referred to by Christ in Matthew's Gospel, chapter 6, verse 22, where He says: "The light of the body is the eye: if therefore thine eye be single, **thy whole body** shall be full of light." Notice that Christ here speaks not about the soul, but about the body. If our spiritual eyesight is properly directed and focused, it admits the healing light and power of God not merely into our soul, but also into our whole physical body.

In speaking about the various avenues by which a teacher can reach a child's understanding, modern educational psychology has coined the two phrases "the ear gate" and "the eye gate." In considering the directions on God's medicine bottle, we find that in this, as in many other respects, God anticipated the conclusions of the psychologists by many centuries. The first direction spoke of "**attending**"; the second spoke of the "**inclined ear**"; the third spoke of the "**focused eyes**." Thus God's spiritual medicine is to be received, with careful attention, both through "the ear gate" and also through "the eye gate." The inward centre of the human personality, at which the two avenues of the ear gate and the eye gate converge, is called in the scripture "the heart." Thus we find that the fourth direction on God's medicine bottle concerns the heart, for it says: "Keep them--that is, God's words--in the midst of thine heart." The very next verse but one of Proverbs--that is, chapter 4, verse 23--further emphasizes the decisive influence of the heart in all human experience, for it says: "Keep thy heart with all diligence; for out of it are the issues of life." In other words, what is in our heart controls the whole course of our life and all that we experience. If we receive God's words with careful attention--if we admit them regularly through both the ear gate and the eye gate-- so that they occupy and control our heart, then we find them to be exactly what God has promised: both life to our soul, and health to all our flesh.

*   *   *

In case this account of what God's medicine will do should seem to some to be mere fanciful theory, I will add here a brief word of personal testimony. Every one of these lessons connected with the healing effect of God's Word I myself have both learned and proved in personal experience. During World War II, while working with the medical services in North Africa, I became sick with a condition of the skin and nerves for which medical science, in that climate and those conditions, could provide no cure. I spent more than one year on end in hospital, receiving every kind of treatment available. For more than four months at a stretch I was totally confined to bed. Eventually, after more than a year, I was discharged from the hospital at my own request, uncured. I decided to ask no further medication or treatment of any kind, but to put the promises of God, in Proverbs 4, verses 20-22, to the test in my own case. Three times a day I went apart by myself, shut myself in with God and His Word, prayed, and asked God to make His Word to me what He had promised it should be--medicine to all my flesh. The climate, the diet, and all other external circumstances were as unfavourable as they could be. Indeed, many healthy men all around me were falling sick. Nevertheless, through God's Word alone, without recourse to any other means of any kind, I received within a short time an absolutely complete and permanent cure.

Let me add that I am in no sense criticizing or belittling medical science. I am grateful for all the good that medical science accomplishes. Indeed, I myself was working with the medical services. But there is just this one thing to say: the power of medical science is limited; the power of God's Word is unlimited.

Furthermore, I would add that there are many Christians of many different denominational backgrounds who have a similar testimony to mine. Just recently I received a letter from a Presbyterian lady who was asked to give a word of testimony in a service in which there were a number of sick people to be prayed for. While this lady was testifying, and actually quoting the words of Proverbs chapter 4, verses 20-22, another lady in the seat next to hers, who had been suffering excruciating pain with a crushed disc in her neck, was instantly and completely healed and delivered--without any prayer being offered--simply through listening with faith to God's Word. The words of Psalm 107, verse 20, are still being fulfilled today: "He sent his word and healed them, and delivered them from their destructions." Christians who testify today of the healing power of God's Word can say as Christ Himself said to Nicodemus, in John's Gospel, chapter 3, verse 11: "We speak that we do know, and testify that we have seen." We can also use, to those who need healing and deliverance, the gracious exhortation of Psalm 34, verse 8: "O taste and see that the Lord is good: blessed is the man that trusteth in him." Taste this medicine of God's Word for yourself! See how it works! It is not like so many earthly medicines, bitter and unpalatable. Nor does it work, like so many modern drugs, bringing relief to one organ of the body, but causing a reaction which impairs some other organ. No, God's Word is altogether good, altogether beneficial. When received according to God's direction, it brings life and health to our whole being.

We have dwelt at some lengths on the physical effect of God's Word, and indeed it would seem not unreasonable to examine with care the nature of a medicine with claims so wide and far reaching.

*   *   *

There now remains just time enough in our study today to examine one more effect of God's Word. This effect is in the realm of the mind. It is referred to in Psalm 119, verse 130: "The entrance of thy words giveth light; it giveth understanding unto the simple." Notice these two effects: "light" and "understanding."

In the world today education is probably more highly prized and more universally sought after than at any previous period in man's history. Nevertheless, secular education is not the same as "light" or "understanding." Nor is it any substitute for them. Indeed, there is no substitute for light. Nothing in the whole universe can do what light does, or take the place of light. So it is with God's Word in the human mind. Nothing else can do in the human mind what God's Word does, and nothing else can take the place of God's Word.

Secular education is a good thing, but it can be misused. A highly-educated mind is a fine instrument--just like a sharp knife. But a knife can be misused. One man can take a sharp knife and use it to cut up food for his family. Another man may take an exactly similar knife and use it to kill a fellow human being.

So it is with secular education. It is a wonderful thing,

but it can be misused. Divorced from the illumination of God's Word, it can become extremely dangerous. A nation or a civilization which concentrates on secular education, but gives no place for God's Word, is simply forging instruments for its own destruction. The history of recent developments in the technique of nuclear fission is one among many historical examples of this fact.

We have often heard people use the expression "darkest Africa." I myself have spent eight years or more in Africa, both as a missionary and in other capacities. It is true that there is darkness in Africa. Yet I have never met an African in greater or grosser spiritual darkness than I was in myself when I had completed seven years of intensive and continuous study at Britain's largest university, and had obtained a position as a teacher of philosophy there.

What changed this darkness in me? Not book learning, or secular education, but the entrance of God's Word. I commenced to study's God's Word simply as a work of philosophy, sceptically, as one who had rejected all forms of religion. Yet before many months, and before I had even reached the New Testament in my studies, the entrance of God's Word had imparted to me the light of salvation; the assurance of sins forgiven; the consciousness of inward peace and eternal life.

* * *

In closing our study today, let me return briefly to a verse which I quoted several times in our previous study, Hebrews chapter 4, verse 12: "the Word of God is quick (or alive), and powerful (or energetic), sharper than any twoedged sword, piercing even to the dividing asunder of soul and spirit, and of the joints and marrow, and is a discerner of the thoughts and intents of the heart."

It will be seen that this confirms and sums up the conclusions which we have reached concerning God's Word. There is no area of the total human personality to which God's Word does not penetrate. It reaches right down into the spirit and soul, the heart and the mind, and even into the innermost core of our physical body, the joints and the marrow.

In perfect accord with this, we have seen in this and in our previous study that God's Word, implanted as a seed in the heart, brings forth eternal life; thereafter it provides spiritual nourishment for the new life thus brought forth;

received into our bodies it produces perfect health; and received into our minds it produces mental illumination and understanding.

*   *   *

In our next study we shall continue to examine yet other operations of God's wonderful Word.

VI
The Working of God's Word

Victory Over Sin And Satan

Welcome to the Study Hour.

Our textbook--the Bible.

Our study today will be the sixth in our present series "Foundations."

To those of you who are joining us for the first time today, we want to say a special word of welcome. We want you to know that in these studies of ours, it is not our purpose to tell you what to believe, but simple to present the scriptures to you in a plain, logical, and systematic way so that you will be able to form your own conclusions as to what the Bible really teaches.

We trust that those of you who have followed with us through the previous studies in this series will by now have formed a new conception of the manifold blessings that become available to you through the systematic study and application of God's Word in your lives.

You will recall that in the previous studies we have worked along the following outline: First, we have seen that the only foundation of all true Christian faith and experience is none other than Christ Himself--Christ encountered, Christ revealed, Christ acknowledged, Christ confessed.

Second, we have seen that once this foundation of Christ has been laid by personal experience in our lives, thereafter we build upon it by studying and applying the teachings of the Bible.

Because of the supreme importance of the Bible in the Christian faith, we have examined the claims which the Bible makes for itself as the Word of God--in particular, the authority which it claims to possess and the practical effects which it claims to produce. We have seen that the ultimate authority behind all scripture, both Old and New Testament alike, is that of the Holy Spirit, the Third Person of the Godhead. This is so because, although many different human instruments were used in various ways to make the Bible available to men, it was the Holy Spirit Himself who worked in and through all these human instruments, and who was thus able to produce an absolutely accurate and authoritative revelation and message of God to men.

Turning to the practical effects which the Bible, as God's Word, produces in those who receive and apply it, we have hitherto examined in order the following five main effects: First, faith; second, the new birth; third, complete spiritual nourishment; fourth, healing and health for our physical bodies; fifth, illumination and understanding in our minds.

* * *

We shall now go on to examine further practical effects of great importance which the Word of God produces.

The next effect which we shall consider is this: victory over sin and Satan.

We have already remarked that probably no character in the Old Testament had a clearer vision than the Psalmist David of the authority and power of God's Word. For an introduction to our present subject--victory over sin and Satan--we may turn once again to the words of David, found in Psalm 119, verse 11: "Thy word have I hid in mine heart, that I might not sin against thee." The Hebrew word here translated "to hide" means, more exactly, "to store up as a treasure." Thus, David did not mean that he had hidden God's Word away in such a fashion that its presence could never be detected. Rather, he meant that he had stored up God's Word in the safest place, reserved for things that he treasured most, in order that he might have it always available for immediate use in every time of need.

In Psalm 17, verse 4, David again gives expression to the keeping power of God's Word, for he says: "Concerning the works of men, by the word of thy lips I have kept me from the paths of the destroyer." Here is a word of direction concerning our participation in "the works of men"; that is, in human activities and social intercourse. Some of these activities are safe, wholesome, acceptable to God; others are dangerous to the soul and contain the hidden snares of the destroyer. ("The destroyer" is, of course, one of many names in scripture for the devil.) How are we to distinguish between those which are safe and wholesome, and those which are spiritually dangerous? The answer is: by the application of God's Word.

One often hears questions asked such as this: Is it right for a Christian to dance? To smoke? To gamble? And so on. The answer to all such questions as this must be decided not by accepted social practice, nor by accepted church tradition, but by the application of God's Word. For instance, I remember that a group of Christian African women students once asked me, as a missionary teacher, if there was any harm in their attending dances at the college where they were being trained as teachers. In reply, I did not offer them my own personal opinion, or the regulations laid down by a Mission Board. Instead, I asked them to turn with me to two passages in the Bible.

The first passage was First Corinthians, chapter 10, verse 31: "Whether therefore ye eat, or drink, or whatsoever ye do, do all to the glory of God." The second passage was Colossians, chapter 3, verse 17: "And whatsoever ye do in word or deed, do all in the name of the Lord Jesus, giving thanks to God and the Father by him."

I pointed out that these two passages of Scripture contain two great general principles, which are to decide and direct all that we do as Christians. First, we must do all things to the glory of God. Second, we must do all things in the name of the Lord Jesus, giving thanks to God by Him. Therefore, anything that we can do to the glory of God and in the name of the Lord Jesus is good and acceptable; anything that we cannot do to the glory of God and in the name of the Lord Jesus is wrong and harmful.

I then applied these principles to the question which those women students had asked me. I said: "If you can attend those dances to the glory of God, and if you can freely give thanks to God in the name of the Lord Jesus while you are dancing, then it is perfectly all right for you to dance. But if you cannot do your dancing in this way and upon these conditions, then it is wrong and harmful for you to dance." I also added, by way of personal experience, that I had been a keen dancer for many years, before I came to know Christ as my personal Saviour, but that I had certainly never done such dancing to the glory of God, or in the name of the Lord Jesus. As far as I know, this answer satisfactorily settled the question of dancing for those students.

Recent researches of medical science have brought to light one very definite way in which many modern Christians, like David of old, have been kept from the paths of the destroyer by the application of God's Word in relation to the use or abuse of their physical bodies. The scriptures teach very plainly that the body of the Christian, having been redeemed from the dominion of Satan, the destroyer, by the blood of Christ, is to be considered as a temple for the Holy Spirit to dwell in, and is therefore to be kept clean and holy on that account. For example, the apostle Paul says in First Corinthians, chapter 3, verses 16 and 17: "Know ye not that ye are the temple of God, and that the Spirit of God dwelleth in you? If any man defile the temple of God, him shall God destroy; for the temple of God is holy, which temple ye are." Again, in the same Epistle, chapter 6, verses 19 and 20: "What? know ye not that your body is the temple of the Holy Ghost which is in you, which ye have of God, and ye are not your own? For ye are bought with a price: therefore glorify God in your body, and in your spirit, which are God's" Again, in First Thessalonians, chapter 4, verses 3 and 4, Paul writes: "For this is the will of God, even your sanctification...that every one of you should know how to possess his vessel-- that is, the earthen vessel of his physical body--in sanctification and honour."

On the basis of these and other similar passages, it is an undisputed fact that many sincere and consecrated Christians have throughout the years refrained from the practice of using tobacco in any form. Until fairly recently it was often suggested by unbelievers that this refusal to indulge in tobacco was merely a kind of foolish, old-fashioned fad, akin to fanaticism, on the part of Christians. However, modern medical research has now demonstrated, beyond all reasonable possibility of doubt, that smoking--particularly of cigarettes--is a direct contributory cause to the incidence of lung cancer. This conclusion of careful research has been endorsed by the Medical Associations of both the United States and Great Britain. In Great Britain, in the last year for which statistics are available, 20,000 men alone died of lung cancer. The incidence of this disease is higher among men than women because over the period of time that it takes lung cancer to develop, a higher proportion of men than women have been habitual smokers. Another undisputed fact, proved by experience and endorsed by medical science, is that death through lung cancer is usually lingering and painful.

In face of facts such as these, the refusal of Christians to indulge in smoking can no longer be dismissed as foolishness or fanaticism. If foolishness can be charged to anyone today, it is certainly not to the Christian, but to the person who regularly wastes substantial sums of money to gratify a lust which greatly increases the possibility of his having to endure a lingering and painful death through lung cancer. And if foolishness can be charged to the victims of this lust, surely nothing short of wickedness itself can be charged to those who, by every means of persuasion and modern publicity, wilfully seek, for the sake of their own financial profit, to bring their fellow human beings under the cruel bondage of this degrading and destroying habit. When we view the facts in this light, I question whether even the slave traders of past centuries, who trafficked for profit in the bodies of men and women, were guilty of causing greater social or moral harm than those who seek financial profit today through promoting the habit of smoking.

Almost exactly the same as has been said about the practice of tobacco smoking applies equally to the practice of excessive indulgence in liquor. It is, once again, a well known fact that a majority of sincere Christians have through the years refrained from this kind of indulgence on the basis of the Bible's warnings against it. Yet it is an equally well established fact that excessive indulgence in liquor is a major contributing factor in many kinds of mental and physical disease and also in the modern toll of road accidents, with their ensuing train of death, injury and bereavement. In this again, as in the case of smoking and its destructive effects, many millions of Christians have been preserved from harm and disaster by their practical application of the Bible's teaching.

With deep thankfulness to God, all such can surely echo the words of David in Psalm 17, verse 4: "Concerning the works of men, by the word of thy lips I have kept me from the paths of the destroyer."

* * *

Not merely does God's Word, applied in this way, give victory over sin. It is also the divinely appointed weapon that gives victory over Satan himself. In Ephesians, chapter 6, verse 17, the apostle Paul commands: "Take...the sword of the Spirit, which is the word of God." Thus, God's Word is the sword which the Holy Spirit uses in the Christian warfare. All the other items of the Christian armour, listed here in Ephesians, chapter 6—the girdle, the breastplate, the shoes, the shield, and the helmet—are without exception primarily intended for defence. Thus, the only weapon of attack which the Christian has is the Spirit's sword, the Word of God. This means that, no matter how carefully or completely a Christian may be armed in all other respects, unless he possesses a thorough knowledge of God's Word and how to apply it, he has no weapon of attack—no weapon with which he can actually attack Satan and the powers of darkness and put them to flight. In view of this, it is not surprising that Satan has always, throughout the whole history of the Christian church, used every means and device within his power to keep Christians ignorant of the true nature, authority, and power of God's Word.

In the use of God's Word as the weapon with which to put Satan to flight, the Lord Jesus Christ Himself is the Christian's supreme example. In Luke's Gospel, chapter 4, verses 1 through 13, we read how "Jesus being full of the Holy Ghost returned from Jordan, and was led by the Spirit into the wilderness, being forty days tempted of the devil." Luke relates how Satan brought three main temptations against Jesus, and how Jesus in each case met and defeated Satan with the same weapon—the sword of God's written Word. For in each case, Jesus began His answer with the phrase, "It is written," and then quoted directly from the scriptures.

It is significant to notice two different phrases which Luke uses in this account of Satan's temptation of Christ and its consequences. In Luke chapter 4, verse 1, we read: "And Jesus being full of the Holy Ghost...was led by the Spirit into the wilderness." But at the end of the temptations, in Luke chapter 4, verse 14, we read: "And Jesus returned in the power of the Spirit into Galilee..." Before His encounter with Satan, Jesus was already "full of the Holy Ghost." But it was only after Jesus had encountered and defeated Satan with the sword of God's Word that He was able to commence his God-appointed ministry "in the power of the Spirit." There is a distinction therefore between being "full of the Spirit" and being able to minister "in the power of the Spirit." Jesus Himself only entered into this second stage of ministering in the power of the Spirit after he Had first used the sword of God's Word to defeat Satan's attempt to oppose Him and to turn Him aside from the exercise of the Spirit-empowered ministry.

This is a lesson which needs to be learned by many Christians today. Many Christians who have experienced a perfectly scriptural infilling of the Holy Spirit nevertheless never go on to serve God in the power of the Spirit. The reason is that they have failed to follow the example of Christ. They have never learned to wield the sword of God's Word in such a way as to defeat Satan and repulse His opposition to the exercise of the ministry for which God actually gave them the Holy Spirit. It may safely be said that no person has a greater and more urgent need to study the Word of God, than the Christian who has newly been filled with the Holy Spirit. Yet, sad to say, such Christians often seem to imagine that being filled with the Spirit is somehow a substitute for the diligent study and application of God's Word. In reality, the very opposite is true. No other item of a soldier's armour is any substitute for his sword, and no matter how thoroughly he may be armed at all other points, a soldier without his sword is in grave danger. So it is with the Christian. No other form of spiritual equipment or experience is any substitute for a thorough knowledge of God's Word; and no matter how thoroughly he may be equipped in all other respects, a Christian without the sword of God's Word is always in grave danger.

The early Christians of the apostolic age, though often simple and uneducated in other respects, certainly followed the example of their Lord in learning to know and use God's Word as a weapon of offence in the intense spiritual conflict brought upon them by their profession of faith in Christ. For example, the apostle John in his advanced years wrote in his First Epistle, chapter 2, verse 14, to the young Christian men who had grown up under his instruction: "I have written unto you, young men, because ye are strong, and the word of God abideth in you, and ye have overcome the wicked one." The apostle John here makes three statements about these young men. First, they are strong; second, they have God's Word abiding in them; third, they have overcome the wicked one (that is, Satan). The second of these two statements is related to the first and the third as cause is related to effect. The reason why these young Christian men were strong and able to overcome Satan was that they had God's Word abiding in them. It was God's Word, within them, that gave them their spiritual strength.

We need to ask ourselves this question: Of how many of the young Christian people in our churches today can we say that they are strong and have overcome the devil? If we do not see many young Christian people today who manifest this kind of spiritual strength and victory over the devil, the reason is not in doubt. It is simply this: the cause which produces these effects is not there. The only source of such strength and victory is a thorough, abiding knowledge of God's Word. Christian young people who are not thoroughly instructed in God's Word can never be really strong and overcoming in their experience.

We are today in grave danger of underrating the spiritual capacity of young people and of treating them in a manner that is altogether too childish. There is even a tendency to create in young people today the impression that God has provided for them some special kind of Christianity with lesser demands and lower standards than those which God imposes upon adults. In this connection, Solomon made a very relevant and penetrating remark in Ecclesiastes chapter 11, verse 10: "Childhood and youth are vanity." In other words childhood and youth are merely fleeting, external appearances, which in no way alter the abiding spiritual realities which concern all souls alike. William Booth's daughter, Catherine Booth Clibborn, expressed a similar thought when she said: "There is no sex in soul." The deep, abiding spiritual realities upon which Christianity is based are in no way affected by differences of either age or sex. Christianity is based upon such qualities and experiences of the soul as repentance, faith, obedience, self-sacrifice, devotion. All these experiences and qualities are the same for men and women, boys and girls alike.

It is sometimes suggested that the way to meet this need of thorough scriptural teaching for Christian young people is to send them to Bible colleges. However, this proposed remedy can be accepted only with two qualifications. First, it must be stated that there is an increasing tendency at present, even among professedly fundamentalist Bible colleges, to devote less and less time to the actual study of the Bible, and more and more time to other secular studies. In Colossians chapter 2, verse 8, the apostle Paul writes: "Beware lest any man spoil you through philosophy and vain deceit, after the tradition of men..." In First Timothy, chapter 6, verses 20 and 21, Paul warns Timothy: "O Timothy, keep that which is committed to thy trust (that is, the truth of God's Word), avoiding profane and vain babblings, and oppositions of science falsely so called: which some professing have erred concerning the faith." These warnings need to be repeated today. In many cases, it is possible for a young person to complete a course at a modern Bible college and yet to come away with a totally inadequate knowledge of the Bible's teachings and how to apply them in a practical way.

The second qualification we must make is that no Bible college course, however sound and thorough it may be, can ever exonerate the pastors of local churches from their duty to provide all the members of their congregations with regular, systematic training in God's Word. The local church is the central point in the whole New Testament plan for scriptural instruction, and no other institution can ever usurp the local church's function. The apostles and the Christians of the New Testament had no other institution for giving scriptural instruction, except the local church. Yet they got the job done more thoroughly than we see it done in most places today. Other institutions, such as Bible colleges, may provide special instruction to supplement the work of teaching done in the local churches, but they can never take their place. The most desperate need of the great majority of local churches today is not more organization, or better programs, or more activities. It is simply this: thorough, practical, regular instruction in the great basic truths of God's Word and how to apply them in every aspect of Christian life. Only by this means can the church of Christ, as a whole, rise up in strength, administer in Christ's name the victory of Calvary, and accomplish the task committed to her by her Lord and Master.

* * *

This accords with the picture of a victorious church at the close of this age, given us in Revelation chapter 12, verse 11, where we read: "And they (the Christians) overcame him (Satan) by the blood of the Lamb, and by the word of their testimony." Here are revealed the three elements of victory: the blood; the word; our testimony. The blood is the token and seal of Christ's finished work upon the cross and of all that this makes available to us of blessing and power and victory. Through the Word, and through the Word alone, we come to know and understand all that Christ's blood has purchased for us. Finally, through testifying to that which the Word reveals concerning the blood, we make Christ's victory over Satan real and effectual in our lives and experience.

As we study this divine program of victory over Satan, we see once again that the Word occupies a central position. Without proper knowledge of the Word, we cannot understand the true merits and power of Christ's blood, and thus our testimony as Christians lacks real conviction and authority. The whole of God's program for His people centres around the knowledge of His Word and the ability to apply it. Without this knowledge, the church finds herself today in the same condition as Israel in Hosea's day, concerning whom the Lord declared in Hosea chapter 4, verse 6: "My people are destroyed for lack of knowledge: because thou hast rejected knowledge, I will also reject thee." A church that rejects the knowledge of God's Word faces the certainty of rejection by God Himself and of destruction at the hands of her great adversary, the devil.

*   *   *

In our next study in this series, we shall continue to examine further operations of God's Word in the life of the believer.

VII
The Working of God's Word

Cleansing And Sanctification

Welcome to the Study Hour.

Our textbook--the Bible.

Stay with us now for the seventh study in our present series, "Foundations."

In the previous studies in this series we have examined the basic foundation of the Christian faith, and we have seen that this foundation is none other than Christ Himself--Christ encountered, Christ revealed, Christ acknowledged, Christ confessed.

Thereafter, the means by which we build upon this personal foundation of Christ in our lives is by studying and applying the teaching of the Bible. Thus, it is the Bible--God's Word--which builds us up in the Christian faith.

In this way, we have been led to examine carefully the nature of the Bible--its authority, and the effects which it produces in those who receive it with the proper attitude of heart and mind.

Considering these effects which the Bible, as God's Word, produces in those who receive it, we have hitherto noted and examined the following six main effects: First, faith; second, the new birth; third, spiritual nourishment necessary for Christian growth and development; fourth, healing and health for our physical bodies; fifth, illumination and understanding for our minds; sixth, victory over sin and Satan.

*   *   *

The seventh great effect of God's Word which we shall now proceed to examine in our study today is that of cleansing and sanctification. The key text for this particular operation of God's Word is found in Ephesians chapter 5, verses 25,26, and 27: "Christ also loved the church, and gave himself for it; that he might **sanctify** and **cleanse** it with the washing of water **by the word,** that he might present it to himself a glorious church, not having spot, or wrinkle, or any such thing; but that it should be holy and without blemish."

There are a number of important points in this passage which deserve attention.

Notice, first, that the two processes of cleansing and sanctifying are here closely joined together. On the other hand, although these two processes are closely related, they are not identical. We may express the distinction between them in this way: that which is truly sanctified must of necessity be absolutely pure and clean; but that which is pure and clean need not necessarily be in the fullest sense sanctified. In other words, it is possible to have purity, or cleanness, without sanctification, but it is not possible to have sanctification without purity, or cleanness. Thus cleansing is an essential part of sanctification, but not the whole of it. Later in this study we shall examine more closely the exact meaning of the word "sanctification".

Turning again to Ephesians chapter 5, we notice, secondly, that one main, definite purpose for which Christ redeemed the church was that He might sanctify and cleanse it.

Paul says: "Christ gave himself for the church that He might sanctify and cleanse it." Thus, the purpose of Christ's atoning death for the church as a whole, and for each individual Christian in particular, is not fulfilled until those who are redeemed by His death have gone through a further subsequent process of cleansing and sanctifying. Paul makes it plain that only those Christians who have gone through this process of cleansing and sanctifying will be in the condition necessary for their final presentation to Christ as His bride--and the condition which he specifies is "a glorious church, not having spot, or wrinkle, or any such thing...holy and without blemish."

The third point to notice in this passage in Ephesians is that **the means** which Christ uses to cleanse and sanctify the church is "**the washing of water by the word.**" Thus, it is God's Word which is the means of sanctifying and cleansing; and in this respect the operation of God's Word is compared to the washing of pure water.

Even before Christ's atoning death upon the cross had actually been consummated, He had already assured His disciples of the cleansing power of His Word which He had spoken to them. For in John chapter 15, verse 3, He says: "Now ye are clean through the word which I have spoken unto you."

We see, therefore, that the Word of God is a great agent of spiritual cleansing, compared in its operation to the washing of pure water.

Side by side with the Word, we must always set the other great agent of spiritual cleansing referred to by the apostle John in his First Epistle, chapter 1, verse 7, where he says: "But if we walk in the light, as he is in the light, we have fellowship one with another, and **the blood of Jesus Christ his Son cleanseth us** from all sin." Here John speaks of the cleansing power of Christ's blood, shed upon the cross, to redeem us from sin.

In order to form a complete picture of God's provision for spiritual cleansing, we must always set these two great divine cleansing agents side by side–the blood of Christ shed upon the cross and the washing with water by His Word. Neither is complete in its operation without the other. Christ redeemed us by His blood in order that He might cleanse and sanctify us by His Word.

In the First Epistle of John, chapter 5, verse 6, the apostle John himself places these two great operations of Christ in the closest possible connection with each other. Speaking of Christ, he says: "This is he that came by water and blood, even Jesus Christ; not by water only, but by water and blood. And it is the Spirit that beareth witness, because the Spirit is truth." John here declares that Christ is not only the great Teacher, who came to expound God's truth to men: He is also the great Saviour, who came to shed His blood to redeem men from their sin. In each case, it is the Holy Spirit who bears testimony to Christ's work--to the truth and authority of His Word, and to the merits and power of His blood.

John here teaches us that we must never separate these two great aspects of Christ's work. We must never separate the Teacher from the Saviour, nor the Saviour from the Teacher. It is not enough to accept Christ's teaching though the Word without also accepting and experiencing the power of His blood to redeem and cleanse from sin. On the other hand, those who claim redemption through Christ's blood must thereafter go on to submit themselves to the regular, inward cleansing of His Word.

*   *   *

"This is He that came by water and blood, even Jesus Christ: not by water only, but by water and blood."

There are various passages concerning the ordinances of the Old Testament sacrifices which set forth, in type, the close association between the cleansing by Christ's blood and the cleansing by His Word. For instance, in the ordinances of the Tabernacle, in Exodus chapter 30, verses 17 through 21, we read how God ordained that a laver of brass, containing clean water, was to be placed in close proximity to the sacrificial altar of brass, and was to be used regularly in conjunction with it:

"And the Lord spake unto Moses, saying, Thou shalt also make a laver of brass, and his foot also of brass, to wash withal: and thou shalt put it between the tabernacle of the congregation and the altar, and thou shalt put water therein. For Aaron and his sons shall wash their hands and their feet thereat: When they go into the tabernacle of the congregation, **they shall wash with water, that they die not;** or when they come near to the altar to minister, to burn offering made by fire unto the Lord: **So they shall wash their hands and their feet, that they die not:** and it shall be a statute for ever to them, even to him and to his seed throughout their generations."

If we apply this picture to the New Testament, we see that the sacrifice upon the brasen altar speaks of Christ's blood shed upon the cross for redemption from sin; while the water in the laver speaks of the regular spiritual cleansing which we can receive only through God's Word. Each alike is essential to the eternal welfare of our souls. Like Aaron and his sons, we must regularly receive the benefits of both, **"that we die not."**

* * *

Having thus noted the process of cleansing through God's Word, let us now go on to consider the further process of sanctification.

First, we must consider briefly the meaning of this word "sanctification." The ending "fication"—f-i-c-a-t-i-o-n—occurs in many English words, and always denotes an active process of doing or making something. For example, "clarification" means "making clear"; "rectification" means "making right or straight"; "purification" means "making pure," and so on. The first part of the word "sanctification" is directly connected with the word "saint"—in fact, it is simply another way of writing the same word..And "saint" in turn is simply an alternative way of translating the word which is more normally translated "holy". Thus, the simple, literal meaning of "sanctification" is "making saintly," or "making holy."

When we consider what the New Testament teaches about "sanctification," we find that five distinct agents are mentioned in connection with it. These five agents are the following: first, the Spirit of God; second, the Word of God; third, the altar; fourth, the blood of Christ; fifth, our faith.

The passages in which mention is made of these various agents of sanctification are as follows:

Sanctification through the Holy Spirit is referred to by both Paul and Peter. In Second Thessalonians chapter 2, verse 13, Paul says to the Christians there: "God hath from the beginning chosen you to salvation **through sanctification of the Spirit** and belief of the truth." In the First Epistle of Peter, chapter 1, verse 2, Peter tells the Christians that they are "elect according to the foreknowledge of God the Father **through sanctification of the Spirit**, unto obedience and sprinkling of the blood of Jesus Christ." Thus, both Paul and Peter mention "sanctification of--or by--the Holy Spirit" as an element of Christian experience.

Sanctification through the Word of God is referred to by Christ Himself. For in John chapter 17, verse 17, Christ prays to the Father for His disciples: "**Sanctify them through thy truth: thy word is truth.**" Here we see that sanctification comes through the truth of God's Word

Sanctification through the altar is likewise referred to by Christ Himself. For in Matthew chapter 23, verse 19, He says to the Pharisees: "Ye fools and blind: for whether is greater, the gift, or **the altar that sanctifieth the gift?**" Here Christ endorses that which had already been taught in the Old Testament--that the gift which was offered in sacrifice to God was sanctified, made holy, set apart, by its being placed upon God's altar. In the New Testament, as we shall see, the nature of the gift and of the altar is changed, but the principle still remains true that it is "the altar which sanctifieth the gift."

Sanctification through the blood of Christ is referred to in the Epistle to the Hebrews, chapter 10, verse 29. Here the author considers the case of the apostate--the person who has known all the blessings of salvation, and has thereafter deliberately and openly rejected the Saviour--and concerning such a person he asks: "Of how much sorer punishment, suppose ye, shall he be thought worthy, who hath trodden under foot the Son of God, and hath counted the blood of the covenant, wherewith he was sanctified, an unholy thing, and hath done despite unto the Spirit of grace." This passage shows that the true believer, who continues in the faith, is sanctified by the blood of the new covenant which he has accepted--that is, by Christ's own blood.

Sanctification through faith is referred to by Christ Himself, as quoted by the apostle Paul, in Acts chapter 26, verse 18. In these words Paul relates the commission which he received from Christ to preach the gospel to the Gentiles, and Christ states that his purpose in so commissioning and sending Paul is as follows: "To open their eyes, and to turn them from darkness to light, and from the power of Satan unto God, that they may receive forgiveness of sins, and inheritance among them which are sanctified by faith that is in me." Here we see that sanctification is through faith in Christ.

Summing up these passages which we have read, we arrive at this conclusion: Sanctification, according to the New Testament, is through five great means or agencies: The Holy Spirit; the truth of God's Word; the altar of sacrifice; the blood of Christ; and faith in Christ.

The process which these facts reveal may be briefly outlined as follows: The Holy Spirit Himself initiates the process of sanctification in the heart and the mind of each one whom God has chosen in His eternal purposes. Through the truth of God's Word, as it is received into the heart and mind, the Holy Spirit speaks, reveals the altar of sacrifice, separates the believer from all that holds him back from God, and draws him to place himself in surrender and consecration upon that altar. There, the believer is sanctified and set apart to God both by the contact with the altar and by the cleansing and purifying power of the blood that was shed upon the altar. However, the exact extent to which each of these four great sanctifying agents--the Spirit, the Word, the altar, and the blood--accomplish their sanctifying work in each believer is decided by the fifth factor in the process--that is, by the individual faith of each believer. In the work of sanctification God does not violate the one great law which governs all His works of grace in each believer--the law of faith--the law which is stated in Matthew chapter 8, verse 13: "As thou hast believed, so be it done unto thee."

* * *

Let us now examine a little more closely the part played by God's Word in this process of sanctification.

First, we must note that there are two aspects to sanctification--one negative and the other positive. The negative aspect consists in being separated from sin and the world and from all that is unclean and impure. The positive aspect consists in being made partaker of God's own holy nature.

In much preaching, both on this and on other related subjects, there is a general tendency to overemphasize the negative at the expense of the positive. As Christians, we tend to speak much more about the "do not's" in God's Word than about the "do's." For example, in Ephesians chapter 5, verse 18, we usually lay much more stress upon the negative "Be not drunk with wine," than we do upon the positive "Be filled with the Spirit." However, this is an inaccurate and unsatisfactory way to present God's Word.

With regard to holiness, the scriptures make it plain that this is something much more than a mere negative attitude of abstaining from sin and uncleanness. For example, in Hebrews chapter 12, verse 10, we are told that God as a heavenly Father, chastens us, His children, "for our profit that **we might be partakers of his holiness.**" Again, in First Peter, chapter 1, verses 15 and 16, we read: "But as he which hath called you is holy, **so be ye holy** in all manner of conversation; because it is written, **Be ye holy; for I am holy.**" We see that holiness is a part of God's eternal, unchanging nature.

God was holy before sin ever entered into the universe, and God will still be holy when sin has once again been banished forever. We, as God's people, are to be partakers of this part of His eternal nature. Separation from sin, just like cleansing from sin, is a stage in this process, but it is not the whole process. The final, positive result which God desires in us goes beyond both cleansing and separation.

God's Word plays its part both in the negative and in the positive aspects of sanctification. The negative aspect is referred to by Paul in Romans chapter 12, verses 1 and 2, where he says: "I beseech you therefore, brethren, by the mercies of God, that ye present your bodies a living sacrifice, holy, acceptable unto God, which is your reasonable service. And be not conformed to this world: but be ye transformed by the renewing of your mind, that ye may prove what is that good, and acceptable, and perfect, will of God."

There are four successive stages in the process which Paul here describes. The first stage is presenting our bodies as living sacrifices upon God's altar. We have already seen that the altar sanctifies that which is presented upon it. The second stage is being not conformed to the world; that is, being separated from its vanity and sin. The third stage is being transformed by the renewing of our minds; that is, learning to think in entirely new terms and values. The fourth stage is getting to know God's will personally for our lives. This revelation of God's will is granted only to the renewed mind. The old, carnal, unrenewed mind can never get to know or understand God's perfect will.

It is here, in the renewing of the mind, that the influence of God's Word is felt. As we read, study, and meditate in God's Word, it changes our whole way of thinking. It both cleanses us with its inward washing, and it separates us from all that is unclean and ungodly. We learn to think about things--to estimate them, to evaluate them--as God Himself thinks about things. Learning to think differently, of necessity, we also act differently. Our outward lives are changed in harmony with our new inward processes of thought. We are no longer conformed to the world, because we no longer think like the world. We are transformed by the changing and renewing of our minds.

However, not to be conformed to the world is merely negative. It is not a positive end in itself. If we are not to be conformed to the world, to what then are we to be conformed? The answer is plainly stated by Paul, in Romans chapter 8, verse 29: "For whom he (God) did foreknow, he also did predestinate **to be conformed to the image of His Son,** that He might be the first born among many brethren." Here is the true, positive end of sanctification: it is to be conformed to the image of Christ. It is not enough that we are not conformed to the world--that we do not think, and say, and do the things that the world does. This is merely negative. Instead of all this, we must be conformed to Christ—we must think, and say, and do the things that Christ Himself would do.

In Colossians chapter 2, verses 20, 21, and 22, Paul describes the purely negative type of holiness and dismisses it as quite inadequate. "Wherefore if ye be dead with Christ from the rudiments of the world, why, as though living in the world, are ye subject ot ordinances (Touch not; taste not; handle not; which all are to perish with the using)?" True sanctification goes far beyond this barren, legalistic, negative attitude. It is a positive conforming to the image of Christ Himself; a positive partaking of God's own holiness.

This positive aspect of sanctification, and the part played in it by God's Word, are beautifully summed up by the apostle Peter, in his Second Epistle, chapter 1, verses 3 and 4, where he says that God's "divine power hath given unto us all things that pertain unto life and godliness, through the knowledge of him that hath called us to glory and virtue: whereby are given unto us exceeding great and precious promises: that by these ye might be partakers of the divine nature, having escaped the corruption that is in the world through lust."

There are three main points to notice here:

First, God's power **has already provided** us with all that we need for life and godliness. The provision is already made. We do not need to ask God to give us more than He has already given. We merely need to avail ourselves to the full of that which God has already provided.

Second, this complete provision of God is given to us through **"the exceeding great and precious promises" of His own Word.** Thus, the promises of God already contain within them all that we shall ever need for life and godliness. All that remains for us now to do is to appropriate and to apply these promises by active, personal faith.

Third, the result of appropriating and applying God's promises is two-fold, both negative and positive. Negatively, we **escape the corruption that is in the world through lust;** positively, we are made **partakers of the divine nature.** Here is the complete process of sanctification that we have described: both the negative escape from the world's corruption, and the positive partaking of God's own nature, of God's own holiness.

The point of the greatest importance is to observe that all this--both the negative and the positive--**is made available to us through the promises of God's Word.** It is in measure as we appropriate and apply the promises of God's Word that we experience true, scriptural sanctification.

In the Old Testament we read that Jacob once dreamed of a ladder reaching from earth to heaven. For the Christian in the New Testament the counterpart to that ladder is found in God's Word. Its foot is set on earth, but its head reaches heaven--the plane of God's own being. Each rung in that ladder is a promise. As we lay hold by the hands and feet of faith upon the promises of God's Word, we lift ourselves up by them out of the earthly realm and closer to the heavenly realm. Each promise of God's Word, as we claim it, lifts us higher above earth's corruption, and imparts to us a further measure of God's own nature.

Sanctification is by faith. But that faith is not merely negative, or passive. The faith that truly sanctifies consists in a continual, active appropriating and applying of the promises of God's Word. It was for this reason that Jesus prayed to the Father: "Sanctify them through thy truth: thy word is truth."

* * *

In our next study in this series we shall continue and conclude our examination of the effects which God's Word produces in the believer.

VIII
The Working of God's Word

Our Mirror - Our Judge

Welcome to the Study Hour.

Our textbook--the Bible.

We are continuing today with our series entitled "Foundations." Our study today will be the eighth in this particular series.

In this series we commenced by examining the basic foundation of the Christian faith, and we saw that this foundation is none other than Christ Himself--Christ revealed and Christ received in the heart and life of each individual believer.

Thereafter we saw that the process of building upon this foundation of Christ in our lives consists of actively studying and applying the teaching of the Bible. Thus, as the apostle Paul tells us in Acts chapter 20, verse 32, it is God's Word, the Bible, which is able to build us up and to give us our inheritance in Christ.

In the last four studies in this series we have examined a number of definite practical effects which God's Word produces in us, as with faith and obedience we receive and apply its teaching. In these four studies we have enumerated altogether seven effects of great importance which the Bible produces. These seven effects are as follows:

Number 1, faith; Number 2, the new birth; Number 3, complete spiritual nourishment; Number 4, healing and health for our physical bodies; Number 5, mental illumination and understanding; Number 6, victory over sin and Satan; Number 7, cleansing and sanctification.

* * *

Today we shall proceed to examine two more main ways in which the Bible, as God's Word, works in the believer.

The first of these ways is that the Bible provides us with a **mirror of spiritual revelation.** This operation of God's Word is described in the Epistle of James, chapter 1, verses 23, 24, and 25. In the two proceeding verses--that is, verses 21 and 22--James has already warned us that, for God's Word to produce its proper effects in us there are two basic conditions: first, we must receive it with meekness--that is, with the proper attitude of heart and mind; second, we must be "doers of the word, and not hearers only"--that is, as we receive the teaching of God's word, we must immediately proceed to apply it in a practical way in our daily lives. If we fail to do this, James warns us that we shall be deceiving ourselves--that is, we shall be calling ourselves by such titles as Christians, or disciples, or Bible students, but we shall not be experiencing any of the practical blessings and benefits of which the Bible speaks. We might sum this up by saying that the Bible works practically in those who apply it practically.

After this warning, James continues in the next three verses as follows:

"For if any be a hearer of the word, and not a doer, he is like unto a man beholding his natural face in a glass: for he beholdeth himself, and goeth his way, and straightway forgetteth what manner of man he was. But whoso looketh into the perfect law of liberty, and continueth therein, he being not a forgetful hearer, but a doer of the work, this man shall be blessed in his deed--or, more literally--in his doing."

In considering this and other similar passages, we must bear in mind that in the English of the King James Version the word "glass" denotes what we today should normally call a "mirror." Thus, James here compares the operation of God's Word to a mirror. The only difference is that a normal, material mirror shows us only what James calls our "natural face"--that is, our external, physical features and appearance. On the other hand, the mirror of God's Word, as we look into it, reveals not our external, physical features, but our inward spiritual nature and condition. It reveals to us those things about ourselves which no material mirror and no work of merely human wisdom can reveal--things which we can never come to know in any other way or through any other means. Someone has summed this up by saying: "Remember that while you are reading your Bible, your Bible is also reading you."

I can still recall, after the lapse of many years, how definitely and how vividly I first proved this in my own experience. I first commenced to study the Bible as a sceptic and an unbeliever--with the background of a student and a teacher of philosophy. I approached it as being merely one among many systems of philosophy in the world. However, as I continued to study it, I became conscious, even against my own will, of certain strange and deep-seated changes taking place within myself. My attitude of intellectual superiority, my sense of self-confidence and self-sufficiency began to crumble. I had adopted the attutude of the ancient Greek philosopher, who said: "Man is the measure of all things." I had assumed that by my own intellectual and critical faculties I was capable of measuring any book or system of wisdom that I cared to study. But now to my own surprise, as I studied the Bible, even though I could not fully understand it, I became conscious that I was being measured by some standard that was not my own, nor that of any human being. Like Belshazzar, in the hour of his feast, there seemed to open up before my unwilling eyes the words: "Thou art weighed in the balances, and found wanting." Without any special change of outward circumstance, I became inwardly restless and dissatisfied. Pleasures and activities of various kinds which had previously attracted and occupied me, lost their power to divert or to entertain. I became increasingly conscious of some deep need within my own being which I could neither define nor satisfy. I did not clearly understand it, but through the mirror of His word, God was showing me the truth concerning my own inner need and emptiness. After several months, this revelation of my need caused me, even in my spiritual ignorance and blindness, to seek God with humility and sincerity. Finding Him in this way, I discovered that He who had thus revealed my need through His **Written Word** was able also to satisfy it completely through the Person of His **Living Word**, the **Lord Jesus Christ.**

Yes, the Bible is a mirror of the soul. But in this, as in its other operations, the result which it produces in us depends to a large extent upon our reaction to it. In the natural order, when we look in a mirror, we normally do it with the intention of acting upon anything which the mirror may reveal to us. If we see that our hair is untidy, we brush it; if we see that our face is dirty, we wash it; if our clothes are in disorder, we adjust them; if we see the evidence of some infection, we consult the doctor for suitable treatment. To receive the benefits of the mirror of God's Word, we must act in a similar way. If the mirror reveals a condition of spiritual uncleanness, we must without delay seek the cleansing which comes to us through the blood of Christ. If the mirror reveals some spiritual infection. We must consult the **Great Physician** of our souls, the one "who forgiveth all thine iniquities; who healeth all thy diseases." Only by acting practically and without delay upon that which the mirror of God's Word reveals to us, can we receive the forgiveness, the cleansing, the healing, and all the other blessings which God has provided for us.

It is just at this point that many people fail to make proper use of God's mirror, to their own great spiritual and eternal loss. Through the hearing or the reading of God's Word, and the moving of God's Spirit, they come under conviction concerning those things in their hearts and lives which are unclean, harmful, and unpleasing to God. Looking thus into the mirror of God's Word, they see their own spiritual condition just as God Himself sees it. Their immediate reaction is one of sorrow and remorse. They realize their need and their danger. It may be that they even go forward to the altar at some church, pray, and shed tears. But their reaction goes no further than this. There is no real effectual change in the way they live. Next day the impresson has begun to wear off. They begin to settle down in their old ways. Very soon they have "forgotten what manner of men they were"; they have forgotten the unpleasant truths which God's mirror so clearly and faithfully revealed to them. Unmoved and complacent, they continue on the way to hell and a lost eternity.

* * *

However, the mirror of God's Word can reveal not only the unpleasant, but also the pleasant. It can reveal not only what we are in our own fallen condition without Christ, but also what we can become through faith in Christ. It can reveal not merely the filthy rags of our own righteousness, but also the spotless garment of salvation and the shining robe of righteousness which we can receive through faith in Christ. It can reveal not merely the corruption and the imperfections of "the old man" without Christ, but also the holiness and the perfections of "the new man" in Christ. If, when God's mirror first reveals to us the truth of our own sin and uncleanness, we immediately act upon this revelation-- if we repent, if we believe and obey the gospel--then the next time we look into the mirror, we no longer see our own old sinful nature, but instead we see ourselves as God now sees us in Christ, forgiven cleansed, justified, a new creation. We are made to understand that a miracle has taken place. The faithful mirror no longer reveals our sins or our failures.

Rather, it reveals to us the truth of such passages as that in Second Corinthians, chapter 5, where Paul describes the new creation in Christ.

For example, Paul says here in verses 17 and 18: "Therefore if any man be in Christ, he is a new creature--or, more literally--a new creation: old things are passed away; behold, all things are become new. And all things are of God, who hath reconciled us to himself by Jesus Christ." Notice that not merely are the old things passed away, and all things made new; but "all things are of God." In other words, God Himself accepts responsibility for every feature and aspect of the new creation in Christ, as it is here revealed in His own mirror. There is nothing at all in it of man's ways or doings. The whole thing is of God Himself.

A little further on, in verse 21 of the same chapter, Paul says again: "For God hath made Him (Christ), who knew no sin, to be sin for us; that we might be made the righteousness of God in Him." Notice the completeness of the exchange: Christ was made sin with our sinfulness that we in turn might be made righteous with God's righteousness in Him. What is God's righteousness? It is a righteousness without blemish and without spot; a righteousness which has never known sin. This is the righteousness which is by God imputed to us in Christ. We need to gaze long and earnestly at this in God's mirror until we see ourselves there as God sees us. We find the same revelation also in the Old Testament, in the Song of Solomon, chapter 4, verse 7, where Christ, the Bridegroom, speaks to the church, His bride, and says: "Thou art all fair, my love; there is no spot in thee." Here the flawless mirror reveals a flawless righteousness, which is our's in Christ.

In Second Corinthians, chapter 3, verse 18, Paul lays emphasis upon the need for Christians to keep continually looking in the mirror of God's Word, for he says: "But we all, with open face beholding as in a glass the glory of the Lord, are changed into the same image from glory to glory, even as by the Spirit of the Lord." Here again, as in James, chapter 1, the modern English for "a glass" would be "a mirror." Thus, we see that Paul, like James, is referring to the mirror of God's Word. He tells us that this mirror reveals to us who believe, not our sins which have been done away in Christ, never to be remembered any more, but in their place it reveals the glories of the Lord, which He is waiting to impart to us by faith. Paul emphasizes that it is while we are thus looking into the mirror and beholding there the glories of the Lord, that the Spirit of God is able to work upon us and to transform us into the very image of those glories which we behold. In this, as in so many other examples of scripture, we see that the Spirit and the Word of God are always ordained to work together in harmony. It is while we look into the mirror of the Word of God that the Spirit works upon us and changes us into the likeness of what the mirror reveals. If we cease to look into the mirror of the Word, then the Spirit is no longer able to work in this way.

In the next chapter of Second Corinthians, chapter 4, verses 17 and 18, Paul returns to the same theme, for he says: "For our light affliction, which is but for a moment, worketh for us a far more exceeding and eternal weight of glory; While we look not at the things which are seen, but at the things which are not seen: for the things which are seen are temporal; but the things which are not seen are eternal." Here Paul teaches that the faithful, victorious enduring of temporal afflictions can produce in us, as believers, results of great and eternal glory; but here again he adds the same qualification as in the previous chapter. This working out of spiritual glory within us is only effective "while we look not at the things which are seen, but at the things which are not seen"--that is, not at the temporal things, but at the eternal. If we once take our eyes off the eternal things, our afflictions no longer produce the same beneficial effects within us. It is in the mirror of God's Word that we behold these eternal things. Therefore, it is in this mirror that we must continue steadfastly to look.

In Hebrews chapter 11, verse 27, we read the scripture's record of how Moses fled from Egypt and endured forty years of exile in the wilderness: "By faith he forsook Egypt, not fearing the wrath of the king: for he endured, as seeing him who is invisible."

Note the source of Moses' power to endure affliction: "He endured, as seeing him who is invisible." It was Moses' vision of the eternal, invisible God and Saviour of his people that gave him faith and courage to endure and to triumph over all his afflictions. The same vision can give the same faith and the same courage to us today. Where shall we find this continuing vision of God in our daily needs and testings? In the wonderful spiritual mirror which He has given us for this very purpose—that is, in the mirror of His own Word.

The secret both of transforming grace and of victorious living lies here--in the use that we make of God's mirror. While we use the mirror aright, God's Spirit works out these effects in our lives.

* * *

It remains to speak of one final aspect of God's Word as it affects our lives, and that is of God's Word as our **Judge.** Throughout the entire Bible it is plainly stated that, by sovereign eternal right, the office of "Judge" belongs to God Himself. This theme runs through the entire Old Testament. For instance, in Genesis chapter 18, verse 25, Abraham says to the Lord: "Shall not the Judge of all the earth do right?" Again in Judges chapter 11, verse 27 we read: "The Lord the Judge be judge this day." And in Psalm 58, verse 11: "Verily He (God) is a God that judgeth in the earth." And in Isaiah chapter 33, verse 22: "For the Lord is our Judge."

As we move on into the New Testament, we enter into a fuller revelation of the motives and methods of God's judgment. In John chapter 3, verse 17, Christ says "For God sent not his Son into the world to condemn the world; but that the world through him might be saved." Again we read in the Second Epistle of Peter, chapter 3, verse 9: "The Lord is not slack concerning his promise, as some men count slackness; but is longsuffering to us-ward, not willing that any should perish, but that all should come to repentance." These scriptures--and many others like them--reveal that God delights to administer mercy and salvation, but that He is relucta it to administer wrath and judgment.

This reluctance of God to administer judgment finds expression in the way in which, as the New Testament reveals, God's judgment will ultimately be carried out. In the first instance, by sovereign eternal right, judgment belongs to God the Father. This is plainly stated by the apostle Peter, in his First Epistle chapter 1, verse 17, where he speaks of "the Father, who without respect of persons judgeth according to every man's work." Here judgment of all men is plainly stated to be the office of God the Father. However, in John's Gospel chapter 5, Christ reveals that the Father has chosen in His sovereign wisdom to committ all judgment to the Son. In John chapter 5, verses 22 and 23, Christ says: "For the Father judgeth no man, but hath committed all judgment unto the Son: that all men should honour the Son, even as they honour the Father." Again in verses 26 and 27 of the same chapter, Christ says: "For as the Father hath life in himself; so hath he given to the Son to have life in himself; and hath given him authority to execute judgment also, because he is the Son of man."

Here it is explicitly stated that the office of **judgment** has been transferred from the Father to the Son. Two reasons are given for this. First, because with the office of judge goes also the honour due to the judge; and in this way all men will be obliged to show the same honour toward God the Son, as they would toward God the Father. Second, because Christ is also the Son of man, as well as the Son of God; that is, He partakes of the human as well as of the divine nature, and thus in His judgment He is able to make allowance, from His own experience, for all the infirmities and temptations of human flesh.

However, such is the grace and the mercy of the divine nature in the Son, as in the Father, that Christ, too, is unwilling to administer judgment. For this reason, He in turn has transferred the final authority of judgment from His own Person to the Word of God. This He Himself plainly states in John chapter 12, verses 47 and 48: "And if any man hear my words, and believe not, I judge him not: for I came not to judge the world, but to save the world. He that rejecteth me, and receiveth not my words, hath one that judgeth him: the **word** that I have spoken, the same shall **judge** him in the last day." This shows plainly that the final authority of all judgment is vested in the Word of God. This is the impartial, unchanging standard of judgment, to which all men must one day answer.

In Isaiah chapter 66, verse 2, the Lord says: "To this man will I look, even to him that is poor and of a contrite spirit, and **trembleth at my word.**" In the light of the New Testament revelation, we can well understand why a man should tremble at God's word. For as we read its pages and hear its teaching, we find ourselves, by anticipation, standing before the last great judgment bar of almighty God. Here, already revealed to those who will receive them, are unfolded all the principles and standards of divine judgment for the whole human race. Of all its judgments, Christ Himself has told us in Matthew chapter 5, verse 18: "Till heaven and earth pass, one jot or one tittle shall in no wise pass...till all be fulfilled." Again

Christ has said, in Matthew chapter 24, verse 35: "Heaven and earth shall pass away, but my words shall not pass away."

In the closing chapters of the Bible, the veil of the future is drawn aside to reveal what will transpire when, in fulfilment of Christ's words, "heaven and earth shall pass away," and God's throne be set for the last great judgment. In Revelation chapter 20, verses 11, 12, and 13, the apostle John unfolds the scene: "And I saw a great white throne, and him that sat on it, from whose face the earth and the heaven fled away; and there was found no place for them. And I saw the dead, small and great, stand before God... and the dead were judged...according to their works." At this last great scene Christ has assured us there will be one, and only one, standard of judgment: the eternal, unchanging Word of God. At this scene will be fulfilled the words of David in Psalm 119, verse 160: "Thy word is true from the beginning: and every one of thy righteous judgments endureth forever." Here will be unfolded, in their absolute completeness, every one of the righteous judgments of God's unchanging Word.

* * *

If we can but see it, this revelation that all judgment will be according to God's Word is a provision of God's grace and mercy, since it enables us here, in this present life, to anticipate God's judgment upon ourselves and thus to excape from it. For this reason Paul says in First Corinthians, chapter 11, verse 31: "For if we would judge ourselves, we should not be judged." How may we judge ourselves? By applying to every aspect and detail of our lives the judgments of God's Word. If we do this, and then by repentance and faith accept God's provision of forgiveness and mercy, God Himself will never bring judgment upon us. Christ Himself makes this clear in John chapter 5, verse 24: "Verily, verily, I say unto you, he that **heareth my word**, and believeth on him that sent me, hath everlasting life, and shall not come into condemnation; but is passed from death unto life." This assurance is repeated in Romans chapter 8, verse 1: "There is therefore now no condemnation to them which are in Christ Jesus."

What must we do to escape God's condemnation? We must hear His Word. In humility and repentance we must accept every one of its righteous judgments, as applied to our lives. In faith, we must accept its record that Christ took our condemnation and suffered our punishment. Accepting these truths of God's Word, we are acquitted, we are justified, we pass out from under condemnation and death into pardon and everlasting life.

All this is through God's Word. Refused and rejected, it will be our judge at the last day. Accepted and obeyed, it assures us already of perfect pardon and full salvation through a righteousness which is not ours, but the righteousness of God Himself.

MESSAGES AVAILABLE ON CASSETTE

SPIRITUAL CONFLICT ALBUM I

1001	How Conflict Began: The Pre-Adamic Period
1002	The Rebellion of Lucifer
1003	Results Produced by Lucifer's Rebellion
1004	The Adamic Race: Five Unique Features
1005	Adam's Fall and its Results
1006	Results of Adam's Fall (cont'd)

SPIRITUAL CONFLICT ALBUM II

1007	Jesus The Last Adam
1008	The Exchange Made at the Cross
1009	Jesus Tasted Death in all its Phases
1010	The Cross Cancelled Satan's Claims
1011	Jesus the Second Man
1012	God's Purpose for the New Race

SPIRITUAL CONFLICT ALBUM III

1013	Five Ways Christ Undoes Satan's Work
1014	God's Program for the Close of the Age—Part I
1015	God's Program for the Close of the Age—Part II
1016	Satan's Program for the Close of the Age
1017	Restraining And Casting Down Satan
1018	Spiritual Weapons: The Blood, The Word, Our Testimony

EFFECTIVE PRAYING

4001	Seven Basic Conditions for Answered Prayer
4002	Intervening By Prayer in National Affairs
4003	Fasting Precipitates God's Latter Rain
4004	Spiritual Weapons For Spiritual Warfare
4005	God's Atomic Weapon: The Blood of Jesus
4006	Epilogue: The Glorious Church

PROPHECY

7001	Climax in four phases: Repentance, Refreshing, Restoration, Return of Christ
7002	Divine Destiny for this Nation (USA) and this generation
7003	Prophecy: God's Time Map
7004	Israel and the Church: Parallel Restoration

- Each Message is approximately one hour in length.
- A printed verse-by-verse analysis and outline is included with every tape.